Heather
Olusi
84.04.04

'You may not believe in Angels but they believe in You'

'Meet your Angels'

By Michelle Fielding

Text Copyright © 2013
'You may not believe in Angels but they believe in You'

All Rights Reserved

The contents of this book may not be reproduced in any form, except for short extracts for quotation or review, without the permission of the author.

This book is dedicated to my daughter Georgia

TABLE OF CONTENTS

How to use this book

Introduction

Awaken to your Divine Gifts

Section 1 - Angelology

Are Angels real?

Angels have no religion

The role of an Angel

Are there fallen Angels?

Questions about Angels

Section 2 – Guardian Angels

Guardian Angels

Who is your Guardian Angel?

Section 3 - Earth Angels

What are Earth Angels?

Earth Angels are Warriors for Love

Earth Angels have their Angel Wings

Earth Angels are Warriors for Compassion

Earth Angels are Warriors for Peace

Earth Angels have their Angel Wings

Earth Angels walk among us!

Questions about Earth Angels

Section 4 - Preparing to meet your Angels

Purify your Home

Purify yourself

Deeper Personal Purification

Heal your Inner Child

Meditation to heal the Inner Child

The Aura – your spiritual coat

Chakras – Spiritual wheels of Energy

Chakra and Aura healing with the Angels

Questions about Auras and Chakras

Grounding

Section 5 - How to connect with your Angels

Meditation-Peace training for the mind

Guardian Angel meditation

Questions on meditation

Angelic Journal

Develop Clarity

Hearts Desires

Write a Prayer

Pray to your Angels

Affirmations

Divine Timing

Manifestation

Questions on connecting with my Angels

Connecting with your Guardian Angel

How to meditate to meet your Guardian Angel

Questions about connecting with your Guardian Angel

Section 6- Angel Signs

How to sense the presence of your Angels

Common Angelic Signs

Angel Sign Experiences

Section 7 - Angel Feathers

Questions about Feathers

Section 8 - Angels and Children

Section 9 - The Angelic Hierarchy

Archangels

Archangel Michael - the master protector

Archangel Raphael - the master of healing and abundance

Animal Healing with the Angels

Archangel Gabriel – God is my strength

Archangel Zadkiel – Righteousness of God

Archangel Chamuel - the archangel of 'unconditional love'

Archangel Uriel – the Light of God

Archangel Jophiel – Beauty of God

Archangel Sandalphon - The Spiritual Journey Begins

Archangel Metatron – the Angel of Ascension

Archangel Azrael – the master of transition

How to use this book

This book has been written in conjunction with the Facebook page 'You may not believe in Angels, but they believe in You'.
(https://www.facebook.com/angels1901?ref=tn_tnmn)
As you follow the instructions and teachings in this book, you can refer directly to the homepage at Facebook 'You may not believe in Angels, but they believe in You'.
This will help you to have a fully interactive experience. Giving you regular guidance and inspiration, allowing you to continue developing your relationship with the Angels.

Please note: For the purpose of following this book with more ease, I have used the words 'your God'. This allows for people of all faiths and cultures to follow the text comfortably. The words 'your God' can obviously be read and replaced by any form of reverence that holds true for you, including: The Divine, The Creator, Universal Energy, Buddha, Allah ….

Introduction

When we first hear about Angels, and become drawn to them, we have many questions. Am I worthy to know an Angel? How do I see, hear or feel an Angel? How do I call my Angel? Should I meditate or pray? Can I ask for help with healing or abundance? Do I need to believe in God to know an Angel?

These questions and much more will be answered in this practical and informative book of how to meet, know and understand your Angels.

This book will show you how to reach your Angels, how to write to them, how to speak to them, and how to feel them through the recognition of the signs and synchronicities, that they will bring to you.

Opening up to your Angels is a profound and life changing experience and for some it is the start of the awakening of a spiritual journey. This spiritual journey will lead some people to higher and higher perspectives about the meaning of their lives.

By reading and following the instructions in this book, you will gain a much deeper understanding, of not only the Angelic realms, but also how they can work with you in each and every moment. The Angels can help you heal on all levels – emotional, physical, psychological and spiritual.

The first step is to just 'ask' the Angels to come into your life. It is not difficult learning to know your Angels. They are reaching out to you and are waiting for you to engage with them. Today is the day that this process now begins for you.

Please enjoy your journey with the Angels. Be sure to write everything down in your Angelic Journal. Over time you will look back and you will see how far you have come. You will see the synchronicities, the blessings, the healings and the miracles that knowing the Angels brings into your life.

Blessings to you all
Michelle

Awaken to your Divine Gifts

Dear Ones, today is the day that you awaken to the Divine gifts of your Angels. Today you can **breathe** the love of your Angels **deep into your heart centre. Then** you can **breathe** peace out **into the entire Universe.**

We are all interconnected; each breath of peace for ourselves becomes a breath of peace for another. Each day open your eyes, open your heart and open your mind. Let the light of your Angels love flood in. See it, feel it, hear it. This is your Divine gift from the Angels.

The more you treat each breath as a gift from your Angels, then the more you appreciate your existence in this very moment. The peace of your mind now, creates peace of mind in your future.

Peace is a Divine gift from your Angels. Angels rejoice when one person finds peace.

Practice peace today, breath in love. Breath out peace.

Where there is peace
There are Angels!

Blessings Dear Ones
Archangel Uriel

Angels rejoice when one person finds Peace

Section 1 - Angelology

Angelology

The study of Angels is called Angelology. The word Angel comes from the Hebrew word Mala'ak, and from the Greek word angelos, meaning messenger. Angels act as messengers, or a bridge between, Heaven and Earth.

Angels are older than civilisation itself and are not associated with any particular religion or belief system. They have been recorded in all mystical traditions, where they are often depicted as the underpinning wisdom.

Earliest Accounts of Angels

The earliest writings on Angels appear in Sumeria, Persia, Egypt and India. These writings gave recognition to the fact, that these winged beings were messengers of God.

Sumeria

In Sumeria, there is a Sumerian stele or stone column, that dates from the fourth millennium BCE. A winged being is depicted pouring the water of life. This winged being is an inhabitant of the Seven Heavens. The Seven Heavens relate to the seven ranks of heavenly beings.

Islam

The teachings of Islam and the Judaeo-Christian tradition have their central ideology around the Seven Heavens. Islam has always had a strong tradition with Angels. It lists Angels and draws inspiration from texts of the Zoroastrians, Babylonians, Assyrians and the Chaldeans.

Bible

The Bible mentions Angels frequently. Archangel Gabriel and Archangel Michael are mentioned by name in the Old Testament.

Archangel Raphael is mentioned in the Book of Tobit or Tobias. Tobit is a book in the Old Testament of the Roman Catholic and Orthodox Bible. Tobit does not appear in the Hebrew Bible and is placed with Apocrypha in Protestant versions.

In the Old Testament, some Angels are described as men in white because they are seen to be clothed in white linen. White Linen is a symbol of immortality to the ancients.

Other Angel Sources

The three books of Enoch are writings rich in angelic lore. The book of 1 Enoch is only in Ethiopic language. Fragments have been discovered among the Dead Sea Scrolls. Aramaic fragments contain the oldest list of angels in existence.

The book of 2 Enoch, also known as the book of Levi, is only found in the language of old Slavonic.

The book of 3 Enoch is in Hebrew. The three books of Enoch were omitted from the Bible. They are quoted by church authorities and in the New Testament.

Kabala

The Kabala is angelic lore drawn from the Jewish mystic tradition. There are two important texts within the Kabala. The Zohar, or 'Book of Splendour' and the Sepher Yetzirah, the 'Book of Formation'.

Summary of the Spheres of Angels

Sphere 1

Seraphim
Cherubim
Thrones

Sphere 2

Dominions
Virtues
Powers

Sphere 3

Principalities
Archangels
Angels
Guardian Angels

The Elemental Kingdom

The Children of the Angels are the Nature spirits. The Nature spirits of the Elemental Kingdom help to create abundance and harmony on Earth.

Devas are evolved elementals, they guard the forests, rivers and oversee the seasons.

Earth Spirits - Fairies, elves, gnomes goblins

Water Spirits - Mermaids and undines

Fire Spirits - Salamanders

Air Spirits - Sylphs

Are Angels real?

'Dear Ones, I approach you from my position in the heavenly peace. Angels are made in the essence of your God. Your God speaks to you through the intuition and love in your heart. When this feels profound it is a moment that can change your life. It is a moment when your Soul begins to become awake.

Angels are our bridge between Heaven and Earth. Your God, makes Angels in his or her essence and sends them on missions of peace to reach you. When you feel those profound feelings of love, peace and tears of joy, then that is the moment an Angel is reaching out and touching your heart. It is in this moment that you know that Angels are real.

As the Angels touch your heart a healing occurs and layers, that may have obscured your true soul essence, begin to be dissolved by the presence of your Angel. Your true soul essence is love. Without the layers to obscure your soul, you can now feel this love. You now know with certainty that Angels are real.

Angels talk to us in the language of love. We feel this in our hearts as intuition and peace. A profound love envelopes us. It is felt as an all-encompassing wave. Quite different to any other experience or situation.

As your heart opens tears of joy may flow spontaneously. Your teardrops are your sign that your Angels do exist. Your heart speaks to you through your emotions'.

Archangel Chamuel

Angels have no religion

Why speak to Angels when I can speak directly to God?

Not all people believe in one God, one source, or one premium place. But Angels can reach everyone. Angels are free from religious, cultural or ethnic boundaries. Angels work as the messengers between Heaven and Earth.

The role of Angels is to spread the beliefs and qualities of unconditional love through their protection, joy, wisdom and happiness.

Angels hold no specific allegiance to any prophet, any religion, or any culture. Angels are free and all encompassing. When a person calls to the Angels, the Angels must respond. This is Divine Law.

If you ask *your God*, the Universe, or Source for a miracle, you will invoke an almighty team. An almighty team of Angelic helpers. Angels are messengers that bridge the gap between Heaven and Earth.

- Angels are made in the likeness of *your God*, or Source, or the Universal Energy
- Angels only know the qualities of Unconditional Love

Angels are free from religious, cultural or ethnic boundaries

Angels – Envoys of Peace

Your God walks with you every day
He sends an Angel as his peace envoy

Your Peace envoy holds your hand
She chuckles at the fun and joy in your life
She skips alongside you, as your dog frolics all around
She holds you while you sleep

Your God has sent you the greatest gift, the gift of Angels
Where there are Angels, there is unconditional love
Where there is unconditional love, there is peace

Angels….. Envoys of Peace

Do different Angels respond to people with different faiths?

The only thing Angels recognise, are the desires or calling from an individual's heart and soul. A genuine request for help and guidance is always heard. The way in which an Angel is seen or interpreted, will be the way you can best understand or receive their message. Angels may therefore appear to you as Male, Female, Human, Animal…. Or any representation of how you understand an Angel to look. For example a bodhisattva.

Angels appear to you in a way you can recognise and understand

Why cant we just pray directly to God? Angels are not deity!

Angels are servants of your God. They are the messengers who guide us between Heaven and Earth. It is not appropriate to worship them. However, Angels create energy that inspires our hearts. This energy causes our hearts to burst open with adoration. It is this feeling of adoration that can be acknowledged. Remember, that the feeling of inspiration from your Angel, is the perfect reflection for you that 'your God' does exist.

Angels do not have free will. You must call upon your Angels to assist you.

Angels can only respond when we call upon them from a position of love, humility, clarity and trust. Always make requests that are positive. Always make your requests for the highest good of all concerned. The Angels will then be able to draw closer to you.

Why cant we just call directly to God for healing?

When you call directly to your God, the Universal energies, or Source, then Angels are sent to help and assist you. Healing occurs when you receive the energy of unconditional love. As such we can ask the Angels for healing as they are themselves beacons of unconditional love.

The main focus should not be on who you are praying to, but more, the intention you are holding in your heart, when you are praying.

The appropriate healing energy that resonates most perfectly for you, will then be brought forward. This maybe for example: the healing energy of Jesus, Angels, Buddha, Krishna, Mohammed .....

When you place your intention within your heart and ask your God, the Universal energy or Source for healing, then the most appropriate healing energy, with which you most strongly resonate, will be brought forward for you.

Healing occurs when you receive the energy of unconditional love

Find Angels, Find your God

It is only in fearlessness that you can find Angels
In finding your Angels you find your God, the Source, and the Divine

Walk your path
In walking your path you find Angels
In finding Angels you find your God, the Source, and the Divine

Call the Archangels and Angels

Archangels and Angels respond to our calls whenever we ask for assistance. Archangels have a particular function to fulfil. For example, *Archangel Raphael is the Master Healer.*
You can also summon Angels and Archangels to help others as well as yourself.

Do the Angels prefer Spiritual or Religious?

Religious

Someone who is religious has a particular faith:
- Believes in a particular God-head or symbol or leader

- Someone who is religious follows only the words, teachings, doctrines of his or her chosen faith
- There is often a ritual of prayer and a specified route to the God-head/source or over-seer of that faith

Spiritual

Someone who is spiritual:
- does not believe in one faith, belief or religion. Instead they embrace the energy that we are all in one Universe and are all at some level interconnected
- does not necessarily believe that any path, leader or doctrine is the route
- may not believe in the concept of Heaven as a place or Hell as a destination
- may believe that the soul continues after death, either coming back to Earth, through re-incarnation, or through serving on another dimension
- may believe that there is more than we can see, touch, hear or smell on the earthly planes
- may believe in other forms of life, including spirit having a continuation of life after leaving their earthly bodies
- may not follow a particular doctrine, script, ritual or leader, but may instead choose a route that is meaningful to them in each moment

Does it matter?

Whether we class ourselves as spiritual or religious, more aspects are similar than dissimilar.
In most faiths and cultures people are driven by a desire, within their deepest being, for there to be peace and love. It is in this similarity that we choose to focus our hearts.

The love of open hearts synchronised towards a common goal, make energies, vibrations and resonance that Angels see and hear. Angels feel these vibrations of our united love; they see them as great beams of light. These beams of love and light help the Angels to fly.

Do not distinguish yourself by your belief; instead distinguish yourself by the love in your heart. Join together with all others who also distinguish themselves with hearts of love.

We are all interconnected. Beams of love and light help the Angels to fly

The words spoken are not important

'Dear Ones, the words spoken about your God are, in and of themselves, not important. The only importance should be on the openness of the heart that speaks them.

In many teachings, there are numerous ideologies about Love, about Healing, about God.
The words used are not of importance. The only importance, is how the words make you feel!

Do not be quick to say 'I believe this or I believe that'. Instead listen to how you 'feel' when you hear or read the words? How do you 'feel' about the words below? How would you 'feel' if your God was saying them to you?

Eternal Love
Angels
Source
Higher Power
Buddha
Krishna
Ascension
Allah
Divine
Ascended Master
Jesus

Oneness
Spirit
Soul
Blessed
Moment
God

How do you 'feel' when you hear the words 'We are all One, we are all interconnected'?

Be sure to read these words and hear and 'feel' them from an open heart. When you use your open heart to see, listen or read, then you begin to understand. You begin to understand, that the words, in and of themselves, are truly inadequate. The words are unable to describe the 'feelings' that you get, when you receive them from a source with an open heart.

There is a need for love, acceptance and unity. When you 'feel' with a closed heart, it is because you are allowing the inception of the ego. With ego you see fear, rejection and separation. With ego you see and feel words as divisive.

The answer is 'do not worry' about:

Someone's words
Someone's viewpoint
Someone's beliefs

We are all uniquely walking our paths of devotion and we are all heading in the same direction. Embrace everyone despite the differing terminology. Instead use your open heart as your barometer.

The greatest teacher of love is your heart
When your heart listens to love, it opens
When it opens the Angels see its light

In that moment the Angels will approach you. They will bathe you in their healing harmonic resonance. Your heart will now begin to heal more and more, deeper and deeper.

All this will occur, because of your acceptance. Your acceptance that your heart is your barometer for unconditional love. Words are not important, only the feelings they evoke when received from and to an open heart.

Read the list of words again, how do they make you 'feel' when you read them again from an open heart'?

Archangel Chamuel

We are all One. We are all interconnected

The role of an Angel

An Angel's role is to try and reach you by acting as a bridge between Heaven and Earth. Angels act upon the instructions and will of your God. Angels teach about unconditional love, peace and joy.

Angels are high spiritual beings who serve, protect and heal us all. When you call upon your Angels, they are already waiting to serve you. Angels are our personal messengers. They are our personal link to Source. Angels help to answer prayers and create miracles!

Angels have their own pathways, as healers, teachers of peace, and teachers of love. Angels have many roles. An Angels presence can however, be felt in many different ways. We can sense them, hear them or see them. We may encounter them during dreams or visions.

Angels can be invoked at any time; we can invite them into any part of our everyday life.
The more you think about Angels the more they will be part of your life. Angels are androgynous, neither male nor female. They are instead created in perfect balance.

Angels have never had a human incarnation, but can temporarily take a human form if help is needed in that guise. Angels are genderless, but will appear to you in the gender or ethnicity with which you can best connect.

Angels can also come to us in the form of animals, including birds, dogs, cats, horses, butterflies …. Our connection with Angels is only limited by our imagination.

We all have a Guardian Angel at birth, who will stay with us during every incarnation. Guardian Angels never evolve into humans.

Angels help to answer prayers and create miracles!

Angels walk with you

Angels are loving, all encompassing, protecting energies, who come immediately to your assistance without condition. Ask your Angels today to walk alongside you as you meander through life's trials and tribulations. Having Angels in your life does not minimise life's ups and downs, but instead shows you how to walk ahead with confidence and peace, despite the changing road.

Your road is your 'gift'. Your road teaches you many vitures; love, peace, patience, compassion..

When you are at a crossroads choose the path of the Angels and your journey will be smoother. You will know that despite everything, you can always manifest peace whatever the seeming external illusions. At the 'crossroads' choose to walk the path with your Angels.

Where there are Angels
There is Peace!

Why cant all people see Angels?

Angels reside on a different frequency to Earth. They reside in a place of finer dimension and resonance. We cannot perceive Angels with our normal vision. They have a faster vibrational rate and are often invisible to the human eye.

Just as each of us is individual, so is the experience for each of us when we invite Angels into our lives. Angels come to us in a manner or form that we will best understand, based on our level of spiritual understanding and our level of peace and love. Some people see, some people hear, some people sense, some people know.

There are many ways of understanding our Angels. If you want to see the existence of your Angel look at your life in more detail. Look more slowly, more deliberately.

When you call an Angel, you will receive a sign or synchronicity. These signs or synchronicities will normally only have deep meaning or relevance for you. Be open to seeing the signs from your Angel and then the evidence of hearing, feeling and knowing will also become bountiful gifts.

The more you train your senses to be in the moment, the more you allow yourself to become calm and peaceful. The more you simplify your life, releasing the dramas, and the attachments, then the clearer the existence of your Angels will be.

Ask an Angel

If you want Angels to be part of your life, then you must ask them to assist and guide you. Your requests are necessary, as Angels cannot intervene without your permission. It is against Divine Law. The Angels can help you with anything and everything.

If you ask an Angel for assistance from a position of trust and sincerity, then an answer will be given to you. You just have to remain open to seeing, hearing, feeling or knowing the signs of their presence. Always finish your requests by saying *'May this or something greater now manifest for the highest good of all concerned'*. The Angels see the higher perspective and so you do not want to limit your requests from your limited earthly view.

Angels cannot intervene without your permission, as it is against Divine Law

Angels teach us in the Language of Love

Love is always the answer
Love is the teaching of Angels
The clear road ahead
The healing road for the Heart and the Soul

Without Love, there is nothing
As nothing exists except Love
Anything that is not Love is Fear

The option to choose love over fear can feel alien at first. Our ego is programmed to give us sensations in our bodies that we call nervousness, anxiety, adrenaline rush excitement, phobias, addictions…. But the reality is that this is just the voice of your 'ego mind'. The 'ego mind' tries to distract you from your true purpose.

Your true purpose is to heal. To heal we need to experience love, unconditional love.

The ego mind is fear, it talks louder when it sees love approaching. Love heals everything unlike itself. Love heals Ego. Ego does not want to be healed. It has been in charge and has been the top dog for so long.

Love will render the ego disabled, diminished, unnecessary, healed!
Love will render your life to peace, harmony, joy… all the qualities of a healed heart
Love is healing. Love is the healing of ego…. Ego is fear…….

Where there is LOVE
There are ANGELS!

Are there fallen Angels?

Archangel Michael heads up an Angelic team which oversees the roles of Angels. Some Angels have been described as fallen Angels. In reality, this is not a true definition. Just as to label something good or bad, would be based on a subjective perspective, or on your level of spiritual attainment.

Angels are messengers of God and as such undertake to work, teach and love unconditionally. This is in line with the Divine Plan or God Mission. However, an Angel may decide not to undertake the work of God.

If this is decided by the Angel even after their initiation into the Angelic realms, then the Angel is no longer able to stay. The Angel has now chosen to work in other realms of existence.

The Angels that leave the Angelic realms have chosen to have free-will. As such these Angels have a choice how to act in their lives. They now have a choice how to react to life's lessons. They have free-will in the same way that humans have free-will.

To have free-will is to forfeit the Angelic Realms. Free-will means that you now operate with ego as one of your driving passions.

Ego helps us to respond quickly to situations, it helps us to compete and aspire to new levels. Ego has to be carefully balanced with compassion and love.

A fallen Angel is effectively someone who has chosen to leave the Angelic realms to experience the workings of choice. They may not have successfully balanced the attributes of ego and unconditional love. This can lead them to make choices which would not reflect the qualities of unconditional love and non-attachment. The qualities normally attributed to Angels.

Angels serve God
Angels are messengers of God
Angels have pure-souls and work only in the realms of Unconditional Love

Angels are made of the Divine Essence of your God , Source, the Divine
Angels have no free will

Questions about Angels

How is an Angel chosen?

An Angel chooses to step forward in front of God after being created by Gods essence. The Angel then asks to serve for the Light. At this point an Angel forfeits free will and serves wholly for the Light.

Are Angels on a continuous path?

Angels are continuously serving humanity. Angels serve as messengers of God and have forfeited free will in order to serve. As the Universe expands its consciousness and understanding, then the light expands. This is reflected back to the Angels as a sign of progress for all. The Angels rejoice as the Light levels expand. The expansion of Light, which is consciousness, helps everything and everyone in the Universe.

How many Angels are there?

There are millions and millions of Angels throughout the Universe. At this time, they are choosing to descend to Earth to help with its progress or Ascension. This is necessary to align Earths energies with the rest of the Universe. It is said that every time a thought of love reaches beyond the Universe, an Angel is created.

Angels have different roles

There are many Angels and they all have different roles. They love to serve. To serve is their purpose. Angels serve by being messengers of God. When you ask an Angel for their help they rejoice.

Angels have many practical skills including healing, finding lost items, and keeping you safe whilst travelling. Angels help us to be happy, joyful and whole.

How can an Angel help me day to day?

Angels can help us in every area of our life. Their help must not however be requested for selfish means, or as a way to bolster our ego. Angels are not a commodity and nothing will happen if you make a request from a stance of manipulation.

When we ask an Angel for their help they rejoice. Angels have many practical skills to help us with the many aspects of our daily lives including:

Angels of Love
Angels of Healing
Angels for travelling – keeping you safe on your journey
Parking space Angels
Kitchen Angels – ask the Angels to bless your food
Angel of lost items
Exam Angels.......
Generally helping you to feel contentment, and allowing you to achieve even higher levels of self-esteem. There is an Angel for everything.

What do Angels do in their free time?

Angels are always in service. Their emanations of pure light and unconditional love are their service to humanity.

Do Angels have feelings?

- Angels do not have feelings in the way we understand or perceive them
- Angels are pure energy, untainted by human emotions, so they only know how to just 'be'!
- Angels do feel pain from situations like war and conflict. But they do not label this
- Angels are beings of Light, they dont label, or distinguish between good or bad
- Angels live on a dimension not comprehensible to us on Earth, there is no time. Existence is fluid from one moment to the next
- Angels have no attachment to the past or the future
- Angels are energy forms of pure unconditional love, free from all ego, labels, attachments, or illusions
- Angels exist in the form 'to be'.

Do Angels cry?

Angels do not cry as they do not feel emotions as we perceive them. However, in situations of hostility, chaos, confusion or war, then light of the Angels contracts. The Angels cannot reach those places or people where the vibrations are hostile.

An Angel is fulfilling its divine purpose when it is able to expand its pure light far and wide. To expand Light for an Angel is equivalent to the feeling of elation in human emotions.

Do Angels make a judgement when I make a mistake?

Angels never make a judgement. Angels only know how to love, protect, heal and nurture with unconditional love. Angels will never leave you. Angels are your 'friends supreme'.

What things make an Angel rejoice?

Angels rejoice at:

The birth of a baby
The innocence of animals
The freedom of the wind

Angels rejoice when our hearts begin to heal and open to the Light. The light of unconditional love.

Do Angels speak to one another?

Angels do not speak to one another verbally. Angels are pure energy forms, which are high vibrating and pure. Angels communicate with each other through the resonance of energy and the harmonics of sound.

Do Angels speak all languages?

Angels do not understand speech in the way we understand language or speech. Angels hear your thoughts and more importantly feel your emotions. They feel your emotions and thoughts like a vibration or a resonance. Angels respond to this vibration with a corresponding sonic or resonance which the individual interprets as language and is then able to understand.

Does an Angel die?

An Angel lives eternally. To die would be to have free will or choice. Angels are pure energy created in the essence of the 'your God'. An Angel can therefore not die as Source is eternal.

Does my Angel go on holiday with me?

Your Guardian Angel enjoys nothing more than going on holiday!

Do Angels have names?

Angels choose names that best suit their role. All names have a sound or resonance and **Angels** choose a name that best suits their role.
Most **Angels** choose names but not all **Angels** have names. The names themselves are not important, only the resonance or vibration of the name when spoken.

Can Angels see good in everyone?

Every soul has the seed of peace and goodness deep within. However, many lifetimes of not being open to the light of Angels, has created layers, veils of illusions, karma and lessons, which remain incomplete.

Once a soul decides to open to the light, having recognised that there is emptiness and a void within, then the layers can be peeled back by the light of Angels. The journey begins.

As the journey begins the layers can be peeled back by addressing previous situations. This creates a healing effect and starts to balance and negate the ego. Some paths are more complex than others. Angels see the seed of peace and goodness within every soul.

How can I serve the Angels?

Our Angel's wish for us is that we find peace. To serve your Angel, find your peace.

What happens to our Angels when we die?

Angels serve us. When we walk from one dimension to another dimension, we are honoured with a rainbow coloured aura and our Angels continue to walk with us.

As we grow spiritually, so do the souls of our Angels grow spiritually. Angels rejoice and are triumphant throughout every stage of your progress on your journey. Angels serve us eternally.

Do Angels wear clothes?

Angels appear to people in whatever form the person can most easily accept. So they may appear to have wings and be ethereal, they may appear in a human form, they may appear as an animal.

Do Angels have wings?

Angels are pure androgynous beings of 'light'. They do not usually have physical wings, but they are often seen as having wings because of the immense luminous light that radiates from their heart centres. The luminous light streams out and emanates in such a way as to suggest that there are indeed physical wings. The halo effect around their head a sign of enlightenment and is again a radiance of 'light' emanating from the heart centre.

How many Angels are we allowed?

The number of Angels around us at any given time will be directly based on the vibration of love we are emanating. The number of Angels will be relevant to our soul needs at that time. There is no limit on how many Angels we can have, as there are literally millions, probably even more.

The more we think, speak and work with Angels then the more healing we experience in our hearts. As we heal, our consciousness becomes finer with the qualities of love and peace. Angels are drawn to these qualities.

Angels also gather closer if we call upon them for their specific Angelic help. There are Angels for all tasks. So the more you ask Angels to help you, the more you heal, and the more Angels will then be drawn to you.

Are my deceased relatives now Angels?

Angels have never had a human incarnation. Any deceased family members will now be residing on a different frequency in the world of spirit. The world of spirit is a different dimension to that of Angels. Nevertheless your family will be around you as they will be helping you and guiding you.

Do I keep Angels from a more worthy person, if I call them?

If you call upon an Angel, remember that YOU are worthy and an Angel WILL hear you.
Angels are pure energy forms, all-encompassing and omnipresent. They are not bound by ego, time or dimensions and can be with all people in any moment.

If you call upon an Angel, you do not deter them from working with another person. Angels are able to work with many people simultaneously. Angels are available to everyone.

Can Angels reach war zones?

In conflicted areas of hostility and war, it is indeed very difficult for Angels to reach the situation. We can help the situation through our prayers and thoughts of peace and love. When we pray our hearts open and the beams of light that expand out can reach the person, the situation or the country you are asking or praying about.

The Angels use the beams of light, created by our unconditional love, to approach the situation. The Angels can get closer by flying on your beams of love and peace and this helps them to reach war zones, which assists them in restoring peace.

No prayers or thoughts of love are ever wasted in the Angelic Kingdom. Every prayer or loving thought is used as a beacon of light to further the existence and process of peace.

Where there is prayer or thoughts of love
There are beams of unconditional love
Angels fly on the beams of unconditional love
Where there are Angels, there is peace

What is it like in the Angelic Realms?

The Angelic realms are like paradise. Everything is pure, everything is light. There are no boundaries or time dimensions. Everything is pure energy, pure resonance with Source. Everything in the Angelic realms is sublime and simplistic.

Beautiful colours and sounds resonate throughout the ethereal realms.
The sound of silence
The focus of infinity
The feeling of weightlessness

All the ways to describe the 'bliss' of being able to access the Angelic realms.

Are all Angels white?

Angels

All Angels are ethereal beings, translucent and white
They are made from the Divine Essence of God
They are omnipresent and can be in all places at all times

Archangels

Archangels work on colour rays or schools of learning
Each ray represents a different set of skills and experiences
Each ray has a different colour

When we call upon an Archangel you will experience the energy ray or school of learning to which that Archangel is assigned.

Angels wear clothes?

Hello!!! I just found your page through someone else who posted something that someone else posted from your page :) pure luck or angel intervention. I have a question if I may? I just started to believe in angels recently :) I was wondering why angels have wings and why do they wear clothes? Do they really need wings n clothes or is it just so we are visually more comfortable with them?

Angels appear to people in whatever form the person can most easily accept. so they may appear to have wings and to be ethereal, they may be human, they may be an animal.

Angels are pure androgynous beings of light. The great emanations of light from their souls are often depicted as them having wings, but in reality it is just the immense light shining out of them....

Can Angels intervene if it is part of our journey to go through it?

Can Angels intervene if it is part of our journey to go through it?

Angels are unable to intervene in the contracts of the soul as this is against divine will.

However, an Angel will protect and guide you through all aspects of your incarnation and will save you if it is not yet your time to pass.

Your soul decides its growth before incarnation and our Angels will help us along our path. They will prompt us to stay on course and provide synchronicities to help us progress.

When we call upon Angels, they help us to walk our journey more smoothly. We will still undergo the same lessons and growth pattern but with the love and protection of Angels, we will see and feel life from a different perspective.

We will choose to see our life from a position of love and not fear. Every perspective we take is based either on love or fear.

Angels teach us, nurture us and protect us so that we only view our journey and the journey of others from a position of love. Angels teach us how to grow and how to heal our heart, through the lessons given by the Soul.

Do all Angels have free-will? (fallen Angels)

You are saying angels have no free will ... how then did Lucifer who was an angel disobey GOD?

I asked the Angels about this and this is what they said 'Angels when created by God have free will.... they have the free-will to serve God, or the Free-will to walk away from the instruction of God. Those Angels that choose to serve God, serve wholly under the instruction of God and no longer choose to have free-will'.

Can Angels draw close when you are depressed and low?

Hi Michelle, is this true, someone told me that if we get low & depressed the angels can't help us?

Angels will come to your assistance whenever you call out to them. Feelings of peace and joy help them to stay with you every day. Feelings of depression don't allow them to draw as close, or to necessarily stay by your side.

However, the Angels will find you help and assistance when you call to them, as this is their job. So help may come to you in more practical terms. You may find a counsellor, or a new hobby that lifts your spirits. You may find a new and fresh perspective. All these things create healing. When you have healing you have peace. Where there is peace, there are Angels.

Section 2

Guardian Angels

Who is your Guardian Angel?

'Dearest One, I am your Guardian from upon high. The height is not a position of hierarchy but a perspective. I along with your God, see your best future plan. The plan that will best serve your heart and soul.

I cannot intervene, but if you call upon me I will allow you to feel the correct path and choices to take. You will know from the strong sense of knowing within your heart and your intuition. This is my voice speaking to you. I cannot intervene unless you specifically request my help with anything and everything.

If it is not your time to pass or does not serve you to have an accident, then I will protect you. At that moment you will experience the wonder of my almighty and unconditional love for you.

Until such a time when you can call upon me, or until I am needed, I walk with you smiling at you with loving eyes. I will be constantly beaming love towards your heart. Every step of the way. I am always reaching out to you Dear One. Please accept my hand. My loving bond for you is eternal. When you feel it, it will be profound'.

Your Guardian Angel

What is the role of your Guardian Angel?

Your Guardian Angel is your personal route to source and your personal connection to the spiritual realms. Your Guardian Angel is your friend Supreme and always looks at you with loving eyes. When your Guardian Angel is around, you will feel profound peace and unconditional love.

The role of your Guardian Angel is to love you unconditionally, to protect, guide and inspire you. To help you in times of need and distress.

Guardian Angels help you to fulfil your life purpose or mission and help you to learn your karmic lessons. They do this by channelling source light towards you.

You are eternally bonded to your Guardian Angel. As you evolve, so does your Guardian Angel evolve? Your Guardian Angel will stay with you during all incarnations.

There are many benefits to knowing or meeting your 'Guardian Angel'. You will have increased confidence in yourself. Your Guardian Angel is the link between you and the angelic realms.

Your Guardian Angel will never interfere with your *free will*, but may encourage and protect you in times of crisis. If in your soul contract you are not supposed to experience pain or you are not yet supposed to die, then your Guardian Angel will step in.

If necessary your Guardian Angel will save you from death or an accident

Your Guardian Angel is available to you in all aspects of your life. Nothing is outside of the scope of what your Guardian Angel can or can't do. You only have to ask them.

Guardian Angel our friend Supreme

Our Guardian Angel is our friend Supreme
Every lifetime, every step, every breath
Always by our side
Protecting us, nurturing us,
Looking at us with loving eyes

Guiding Angels

In addition to your Guardian Angel you also have one or maybe several guiding or helping Angels. They work with your Guardian Angel and their job is to assist you with your spiritual lessons. As you evolve your guiding angels may change. Your Guardian Angel however, remains with you eternally.

Guardian Angel Love is eternal

Once you have recognised your connection with your Guardian Angel, it is there for eternity. It can never be severed or lost. In those times where you feel that you no longer feel your Angel, it is the voice of the ego mind, of fear.

Say **'Angel Dear One, please show me how to love and to reconnect with your essence'**

The Angels will step forward beaming brightly. Angels always look at you with loving eyes. Their love has never gone away, but the illusion of the ego mind, created a fear. In that moment fear hindered your Angel from drawing close.

Keep your attention on your Heart and still the mind. In the stillness, in the calm the love of your Angels wings you will again find.

I am your Guardian Angel

I am your Guardian Angel dear child, an overseer of your soul
I lift you to be at Heavens side

When I look at you, you fill my heart with pride
Every dawn till dusk, I endeavour to be your heavenly guide

God has instructed me, you see
To be a beacon of 'unconditional love' for you eternally

No bounds of ego, do I know
Only pure light and love, inside my soul

Is our Guardian Angel with us when we are in the womb?

Your Guardian Angel is with you during all incarnations, from the moment you are created by the essence of 'your God'.

Your Guardian Angel is also with you:

During your wait to choose your parents
In the womb and during your birth
During your lifetime
At death
During Bardo.... and then the cycle begins again

What is the difference between my Guardian Angel and a Spirit Guide?

Guardian Angels are sometimes referred to as spirit guides, but this is actually not accurate.

The role of a Guardian Angels

Everyone has a Guardian Angel. This Angel stays with you constantly during your entire lifetime and beyond.

Your Guardian Angels love for you is unconditional
Your Guardian Angel protects you and keeps you safe
Your Guardian Angel has never had a human incarnation

The role of a Spirit Guides

A spirit guide is a loving being who has lived before as a human being on earth
This person upon death will have received training on how to be a spirit guide
A spirit guide will not interfere with your free will or make decisions for you
Your spirit guide may have been a grandmother, parent, sibling or beloved friend or may not have been known to you in your lifetime.
Your spirit guide may have passed away before you were born.

Your Guardian Angel Walks with you

*Your Guardian Angel walks with you
Through every incarnation
Through every stage of your life
Through every thought and emotion*

*Take time today to meet your Guardian Angel
Your Guardian Angel is your Friend Supreme*

Speak to someone elses Guardian Angel

You can ask that your child's **Guardian Angel** protect and walk closely with him or her every day. **Send** feelings of **love, healing and joy** to your children and they will be protected by your positive bubble of energy.

Your **thoughts of love** will create the energy for their **Guardian Angel** to move even closer to them and to make a stronger connection. Your thoughts are very powerful. It is the thoughts of **love** that **heal others.**

Ask the **Guardian Angel** of your friends, family and people in need to protect them throughout their day

QUESTIONS ABOUT GUARDIAN ANGELS

I need an Angel to help me build my relationship with my eldest daughter My oldest daughter needs an Angel to build our relationship. I love and miss her.

In situations like these you can speak to your Guardian Angel about this matter. You can ask your Guardian Angel to go and speak to the Guardian Angel of your daughter.
- Go to your sacred space in your home. Relax you entire body
- Then with your Angelic Journal, write down everything that you want to say to your daughter. Say everything that is in your heart. Remember tears are healing for the soul.
- Now ask your Guardian Angel to tell your daughter's Guardian Angel how you feel

Take a breather. In your next session I would like you to relax and in your Angelic Journal you can start to write again:
- How would your relationship with your daughter look it if were healed and she were with you right now? For example you can say *'the relationship between me and my daughter is now healed on all levels and we enjoy quality time together, chatting, laughing, growing'*
- Keep writing down how this relationship would look if you had it now and how you feel about it
- Ask your Guardian Angel *'May this or something greater now manifest for the highest good of all concerned'*
- Thank your Guardian Angel
- Release this now to the Angels and allow them to take this to the heart of God

In the next session:
- Call in Archangel Michael
- Ask Archangel Michael to cut any cords of fear, or patterns that no longer serve you in regard to how you relate to your daughter

- Feel it as he brings down his sword releasing you from the cords that have created patterns of thought or behaviours that have kept you stuck in negative programming
- Now ask Archangel Chamuel to come in and to bathe your heart in the pink light of unconditional love. Let this pink light bath all your heart. Allow it to overflow and flood the whole of your body
- When you are fully filled in the pink light of unconditional love imagine a beam of this light going from your heart directly to the heart of your daughter. Imagine this pink light totally bathing her heart
- Thank Archangel Michael. Thank Archangel Chamuel
- Write everything down in your Angelic Journal
- Go about your day and your life knowing that with Divine Timing your new relationship with your daughter will manifest

Is my son my Guardian Angel?

I was wondering something about guardian angels. My 6 year old son died in 2001 due to a car accident. I was wondering if it were possible that he is my guardian angel. I don't know if that's possible but I feel like he is. But what I am gathering from this page I could have more than 1 angel??

Hello, there are many Angels and there are also Archangels. They all have different roles. There is an Angel for everything we need help with, we only have to ask.

Then to make things even more amazing we all have a Guardian Angel that is with us throughout every incarnation, as we evolve they evolve.

Angels have never had and never will have a human incarnation. Your son will no doubt be around you, but he will be with you in spirit, and may even be your spirit guide. All spirit guides have had a human incarnation.

To make your relationship stronger with your Guardian Angel then follow the instructions on how to meet your Guardian Angel meditation, in the meditation section of this book.

For all the other Angels just ask for what you need. Angels cannot intervene unless you request their help, except on those occasions where it is not your time to pass. Then your Guardian Angel will save you. If you want to know about your son, just ask your Guardian Angel about your son.

Your Guardian Angel will hear you , and will give you a sign. Please come back to me if you need further help. Our loved ones are eternally bonded to us, on all levels of our journey. Blessings dear one... Michelle

Should I be cautious with my Guardian Angels name?

I was taught to be careful sharing the actual name of spiritual guides, so I figured why not just be cautious with my Guardian Angels name? Do people have more than one Guardian Angel?

There is a difference between spirit guides and Angels, and the message you have received in the past will have most definitely of been from spirit and not from an Angel. I say this because you would not have felt the need to be careful in saying or expressing the name in the way you describe.

Angels only know love and peace and do not in any way create fear or caution in the way you describe. An Angels guidance will only ever sound and feel subtle and loving, and will never tell you what to do.

You have one Guardian Angel all your life and spirit guides come and go depending upon your stage spiritually and what you still may need to learn.

Before you begin any meditation it is important to always ground yourself and to call in an Archangel such as Archangel Michael to protect you. Do not rush the grounding and protection process. When your Angel comes to you, you will definitely see a big difference in your life. Your Angels presence is profound and life changing. You will be very happy to tell people all about your Angels name.

Does my father have an Evil Guardian Angel?

My father is so unkind and hostile and yet he seems to be protected while I am persecuted? Does my father have a dark soul? Is that possible?

Your father's soul is teaching you. At the time of your incarnation it would have been agreed between you and your Guardian Angel, who and what would help your soul to grow and evolve.

Your father will have an all loving Guardian Angel as we all do. His Guardian Angel will always be there alongside him. Angels cannot however intervene with soul contracts; they can only continue to love us unconditionally without judgement.

Yours is a soul that has decided to take these lessons from your father as initiations. These circumstances are helping you to learn about forgiveness, compassion and clarity. Decide what you intend to learn from your experiences.

Say 'I am a child of God, I now surrender. I ask you to show me the way. Angels, please take my hand and walk with me. I now release all that no longer serves me. I am now totally healed on all levels, emotional, physical, psychological and spiritual'.

Now thank your Angels.

With your Angelic Journal take some time to identify what qualities, skills and strengths you have gained due to your experiences:

- If you have been rejected, then you now know how to love unconditionally
- If you have been abused, then you now know and are constantly learning, how to stand up with courage and dignity
- If you have been lonely, then you now know how to be alone, whilst standing in your power. You understand the greatness of being in the moment
- If you have been afraid, then you now know how to listen to the power of your intuition
- If you have been lied to, then you now know how to speak with truth, honesty and integrity
- If you have felt powerless, then you now know how to find your inner strength

All these qualities, unconditional love, courage and dignity, being in the moment, intuition, truth, honesty, integrity and inner strength. All these qualities, are the qualities of a Spiritual Warrior, a Child of God.

Focus your healing efforts on sending love to your 'inner child', through meditation, visualisation and affirmations. Pray and walk along your path one moment at a time.

Say 'I am a Child of God. This moment is the first moment of the rest of my life'

Let the Angels into your life. Ask them to be with you in each moment, to sing with you, to swim with you, to run with you, to jump with you. Ask the Angels to show you that you are very loved in each and every moment. As things begin to change, remember to thank your Angels.

Meeting your Guardian Angel is profound

Thank you Michelle. I have been smiling so much lately that I almost feel silly. The other day one of my grandchildren told me 'Grandma, you seem so much happier now'. I told her it was because my heart is so full of love that it cannot hold it all so it bursts out in smiles. She was right, I am happier, more serene, than I have ever been. Many years wasted with sadness, worry and grief but that is all past, forgiven, forgotten. Any time I think about the bells I can hear them. They bring with them a very calming feeling. Now, I am finding pennies and feathers everywhere. Not just one penny but several in one spot. Huge feathers, like the tail feathers of a turkey. What is best of all is once again seeing things as if through the eyes of a child, the simple things, the beautiful things. Flowers seem to have more colour, more vibrant. Beautiful butterflies. Looking deeply into the eyes of animals – I cannot even explain how that feels, just that they are so full of love. And yes all of it makes me smile ☺ I am overjoyed that I feel as though I have reached a whole new level. I am so blessed that Walden has made himself known to me. I look forward to the time when Walden and I can carry on a conversation. Many thanks for your guidance and help. Blessings.

Section 3

Earth Angels

What are Earth Angels?

Earth Angels are people who, under the influence of the Light of their God, carry out missions of peace. Earth Angels are those people that just seem to be there in your time of need.

An Angel, will sometimes manifest as an Earth Angel to help someone during a crisis, when they hear cries from a person's soul. Angels can appear to us, and come to us, in whatever form we are most easily able to understand. They can appear in human form, as animals, birds, butterflies even insects!

The label Earth Angel is frequently given to those people, who in their day to day existence use their intention and intuition, to work with the light and love of Angels to help others.
They therefore display the qualities of the Angels.

Angels often use these compassionate beings to channel their loving energy and assistance, to those situations or places, where the frequency is too dense or hostile. Angels find it difficult to reach people and places where there are discordant energies.

An Angel Footprint

Where an Angel has walked, there is an energetic footprint
As the next person passes by, this energy is then absorbed

Where an Earth Angel walks there is an energetic footprint
As the next person passes by, this energy is then absorbed

As your raise your awareness, you raise your vibration
You find your wings. Your energy becomes finer and purer

Your footprint becomes more unique and subtle
Walk with your Angels today, make pure footprints in the ground

Help the soul of another to be nurtured and grow
We all grow together, we are interconnected

How to be an Earth Angels

Earth Angels are kind. Be an Earth Angel, show a random act of kindness today. Love is the only thing that everyone needs. Take up some voluntary work and choose a life where you can work in service to others. Imagine how an Angel would undertake his or her day. Mimic these qualities until they become second nature for you.

Smile at a boisterous child
Buy some flowers and give them to your boss
Take out the rubbish for your neighbour
Bake a loaf of bread for your elderly neighbour
Say something kind or inspiring to the person sitting next to you on the way to work
Ask the single parent in your road if they need any help this week with anything
Give your pet some extra attention
Make your own sandwiches and with the money you save buy YOURSELF a nice gift
Look at that homeless person, with the eyes of God and a heart of Love. Know that your loving thoughts and good intention can help that person to turn their life around.

A kind soul is inspired by Angels – You can't give without receiving

Be an Earth Angel today

Be a worker for heart centred love today
Spread your wings and help another to fly!

Show some kindness
All around you are people in need

Reach out with your Heart filled with Compassion
Everyone has their own story
Everyone has their own path to explore

Everyone is growing
Everyone is learning
Be an Earth Angel today!

Step forward and reach out

As you step forward have clarity, courage, faith and strength. These qualities and many more will be provided to all Earth Angels. Show others how the Angels support, love and nurture you.

Today you can be an example and you can show people how to step forward with their own Angels. All way showers are blessed by the light and love of Angels. Step forward today.

Be an Earth Angel today, go forth and reach out! Reach out to a fellow person of your community. Nurture them through your love, compassion and service.

Earth Angels reach out

*As you climb your **spiritual path**, you will know that sometimes the road is not smooth.*
As you climb your spiritual mountain you will know that sometimes the path can become suddenly steep and narrow.
As you climb the ascension ladder, you will know that every step is a step closer to God.

Every meander, every crag or rocky crevice, every rung on the ladder, eventually leads you to the 'plateau of peace'. Earth Angels say 'Take my hand, I know this part really well'.

When you arrive you will look back and you will reach out to the next person coming up behind...... You will say: 'take my hand, I can help you, I know this part really well'

When you are leading from the front
When you are walking blindly in a storm
When your feet and emotions feel numb from the journey

Then it is your turn to look forward and in front you will see a hand. It is the hand of Gods' team. It is your Angel who will now say: 'take my hand, I can help you, I know this part really well'

As you walk your **spiritual pathway** you are both in front and behind, but each one of you is a **'link'** that connects to another.

As one person learns, another person teaches
As one person follows, another person leads

You will ascend towards **God,** one by one, but you ascend with the help of each other.

Ask your Angels to help you be the best **'link'** in the chain of **'Ascension'**, that you can possibly be!

Earth Angels are Warriors for Love

Earth Angels have open Hearts

Open your heart and let the love of your Angel find you. Open your heart and reach out with compassion. Someone somewhere needs to feel your compassion in order to take the next step. Reach out to someone today and show them how your love and compassion can help them to move forward.

Love heals everything unlike itself. Ask the Angels to show you how to feel more compassion, not only for yourself, but also for others. It is in the giving that we receive.

Say 'Angels, Please help me to open my Heart wider, to heal deeper, to love longer'

Everyone is doing the best that they can with the amount of wisdom their soul currently holds. From this point of understanding we are able to have more compassion, more love, more forgiveness. We recognise that everyone is right, when looking out from their own current perspective.

A person with a closed heart will have a different perspective to that of a person with an open heart. The more open the heart, the higher and more encompassing a person's perspective will be.

No one is right and no one is wrong. Everyone is just where they are at this time. Each day serve by opening your heart just a little wider.

Say *'Angels, please help me to have a higher perspective based on love, joy and peace. Please help my Heart to open wider, to heal deeper and to love longer'*

The work we do to heal and open our Hearts, in turn, affects the whole. As one heart begins to heal, it sends out a resonance of Love. This resonance travels out and touches everyone and everything that it reaches.

This resonance may be enough this time to create a stirring in the heart of someone. Someone, who has to date, not heard or felt the energy or resonance of unconditional love around them.

This day may be the day their soul hears their 'awakening' call. Today, the healing of your heart, may create the awakening in another's heart. Others may now start to experience the gifts of unconditional love, peace and joy.

Your opened heart, sent all these qualities as a gift ... in just one heart beat! When we open our hearts wider, we open the hearts wider for all, for eternity

The Angels see hearts that are opening and they fly in on its beams of love, they reach you.
Have an Angel reach you today. Open your Heart... and let the **Love of your Angel** find you.

Diamond Heart

Your heart is like a gem, a crystal. It has many facets.

Polish your heart as it is like a diamond.
It reflects the many aspects of your unconditional love, for yourself and others.

Polish your heart by speaking your truth, acting with integrity and showing compassion, towards yourself and others.

The world is rapidly changing and a polished heart is a loving heart that can lead, cherish and protect others.

Today is your day to shine
Embrace your Glory
Show others the benefits of acting with integrity

Where there is a shining heart
There are Angels!

An open heart

When a heart opens it brings in more love, more light. This is the love and light of your God. As the love and light expands, it is all encompassing. It flows out greeting everyone you meet.

Your energy of love, from your open heart, heals everything in its path. Every embrace, from your heart of love, helps another. Others begin to find and feel love. Others begin to feel your peace. This peace is your gift. They want to feel it too. What greater gift than your gift of peace.

Where there is peace
There are Angels!

An abundance of love

An abundance of love creates an abundance of Peace.

Where there is an abundance of Peace
There is an abundance of Angels.

Be abundant….
Repeat this mantra: Love, Peace, Angels

LOVE, PEACE, ANGELS, it must be said

LOVE, PEACE, ANGELS, the only way ahead

Look around you, there are people in need

Now is your time to shine
Now is your time to abandon false ideas about wealth, possessions and power

Replace these illusions with love – unconditional love
Look around your work place, your community, your country, your Universe

Make the first step today!

One smile, can change another person's day
One word of encouragement can change a person's life
One hug, can heal a person on many levels

Be the peace you want to see
Be the love you yourself want to feel
Be the change!

Where there are the qualities of: Boldness of action, an open heart, harmlessness, truth, there is a team of Angels waiting to help you

Together we create an Almighty Team
Together we create Peace
Together we create Change

Reach out to others today. Be a warrior for Love.

Where there is Love
There are Angels!

Love – the souls perspective

A viewpoint is your individual perspective, based on your own learning, self-love and learned fears. To see things as they truly are, release your fears, open your heart to others and have compassion for everyones' stage on their personal journey.

When your soul reaches the end of this stage in its journey, then it will gain a higher perspective. It will view everything very differently, seeing the whole, bigger picture.

Try to release your held beliefs and be open to viewing things a different way. From the soul's perspective. In releasing your fears, you are saying to your God, that you accept the love of God and it will be forthcoming.

Nourish your Soul with Love

Nourish your soul with love, peace and contentment. Seek for a deeper understanding of yourself in relation to others.

Love yourself
Love others
Love begins in a moment
One step
One Breath
One small realisation that everything is interconnected

Life is interconnected, your soul is my soul and my soul is your soul. Lets nurture each other with care and love every day.

The Angels rejoice when we recognise the worthiness of another soul needing heart felt love.

We cannot give without receiving, so always give openly, honestly and lovingly. The way of the Angels, your Gods way.

Everything that is nurtured grows

It is in the giving that we receive

It is in the believing that we hear
It is in the light that we see
It is in the Love of our Angels that we flourish
Everything that is nurtured grows!

Earth Angels are Warriors of Compassion

What is Compassion?

Let us consider the eternal life of the soul. It has many lives, in different forms, as it grows and matures.

It is possible that we have all experienced many thousands of re-incarnations, over many lifetimes. It is possible that the person who you find annoying, unkind or your enemy, may in actual fact, have been your child or your mother in a previous life?

Is it not normally the case that we generously extend the emotion of compassion, to our mother and our child? That we extend the emotion of compassion regardless of what actions they may or may not have taken?

Just for today offer compassion to everyone you meet. Greet and treat everyone as if they were your own mother or child. Just for today treat yourself with the love, that your own mother or child, would extend to you.

Release the Anger – have compassion

Anger is the passion that clouds reality and gives a false sense of 'I am right and you are wrong'! At this crossroads there can be no Peace.

Release your need to be right
Release your need to feel hurt
Release your need to feel betrayed

In the eyes of the Angels the perspective is totally clear and the way forward is crystal;

Forgive yourself
Forgive others
Have Compassion for yourself
Have Compassion for others

The way forward is clear.
The way forward is NOW!
The way forward is unconditional love for yourself and others

Are you practising Compassion or Compulsion?

Compassion is the giving of energy for what people need
Compulsion is the giving of energy for what YOU need

Be compassionate to yourself and others, only give and receive those things that people need. Then let them take the initiative to do their own internal work.

To impose your compassion and generosity would be to deny their learning and growth in that situation. This growth will have been decided at a soul level before incarnation.

To impose generosity and to try to take away their spiritual growth is to create karma for you. Compassion is seeing everyone with the eyes of God and a heart full of Love.

When you next help a homeless person, help them from the perspective that your energy will help them to move forward. Your energy will help them to find their wings. Compassion does not mean you fly for them.

The Beggar Man

The hungry man sits with his tin ajar
People cross his path
Some just stare

Angels! The man sighs
This is not my Life!

In a moment of hearing the souls' cries
The Angel of the Divine arrives

'Dear Soul, take my hand, take it dear man. Stand up tall, I will never let you fall. Let me take you to a warm and nurturing place'

The Angel points to the man's own Soul, whilst taking time to touch his face
In a moment the Angel's vision has gone
But the Love and the profound moment , for this man, will eternally linger on

Reach out your hand and also act Divine
Don't just give a dollar, but give the man a moment of your time

Give the beggar man, another reflection of the Divine

His Soul will heal and in his awakening and new belief in himself
The Angel's Love will help him to continue on with stealth

Show some kindness

All around you are people in need
Reach out with your heart filled with Compassion

Everyone has their own story
Everyone has their own path to explore

But someone, somewhere needs to feel your compassion, in order to take the next step. Reach out to someone today and show them how your love and compassion can help them to move forward.

Ask the Angels to show you how to feel more compassion, not only for yourself, but also for others. It is in the giving that we receive.

Love heals everything unlike itself

Make a shower of Compassion, Love and Understanding

We can all only walk on the path that we currently understand. In the direction, that we are currently facing. With the knowledge we currently hold.

But at each 'crossroads' the Angels are waiting. As we learn more we walk onto a higher path everything we have previously experienced is now below us

Looking down at the path below you, see the others. Shower them on their current path of experience with the energies of compassion, love and understanding.

Those on the path above you will be doing the same, so there is always enough love to go around.

As you look below you, you see others in their daily struggle to understand from their present perspective. Continue to send them a shower of energies, compassion, love and understanding.

You smile! You are smiling because you know that with your loving shower of compassion, love and understanding, they can and will succeed in walking to higher ground.

You smile because you can now forgive yourself and others. You can see quite clearly everyone's unfolding path and journey.

You turn and look forward, you feel elated, joyful and optimistic. You walk confidently one step firmly in front of another. From this position of fresh perspective there is forgiveness.

Thank your Angels as you walk
Thank your Angels as you smile
Thank your Angels, the way ahead is clear.

Earth Angels are Warriors for Peace

What is Peace?

Peace is a healed heart. To heal your heart, call in the Angels every day and absorb their love, healing and wisdom.

Your Angel will heal you by peeling back one layer at a time. One layer of stuck or negative energies within and around your heart. These stuck energies can be at an emotional, physical, psychological or spiritual level.

With each layer removed, you are better able to hear the voice of your God and the love of the Angels. When you are spiritually healed you are complete.

Where there is healing
There are Angels!

Realise your true potential. Your true potential as a giver of Peace. Peace is your gift. You can enfold everything and everyone in your thoughts of Peace, they will feel it. Peace is an all-encompassing energy, that heals people on deep levels, conscious and subconscious.

People will be drawn to your essence. They will be drawn to the love and peace in your heart.

Today, share this love and peace in your heart
There are no greater gifts

Give your love freely, enabling another to feel Peace. Be the love and peace you want to see. Great Blessings are bestowed upon those that bring Peace to the masses.

Be a way-shower
Be a Beacon
Be a symbol of Peace

An abundance of love creates an abundance of peace
Where there is an abundance of peace
There is an abundance of Angels!

Be abundant, repeat this mantra – 'Love, Peace, Angels' – and Angels will walk with you!

Fear – the illusion preventing Peace

Where there is fear, there is illusion. Illusion is created by lack. A lack of light into the centre of your heart. The seed of Love in your Heart needs the light.

Ask the Angels to help you absorb more light, so that the seed of love can grow even stronger. Take the Light and the Love from your Angels, know that in receiving you are now able to give tenfold. Everything is interconnected. We are all nurturing and healing and loving each other. We are all the link in the chain to Peace.

Where there is Peace
There are Angels
Repeat this mantra: 'Love, Peace, Angels'!

Higher Perspective

Today is your day, reach up to the moon
The stars, and the Universal skies

Let your fingers feel the flutter of an Angel's wings as it floats by
As you reach ever upwards know that your heart rejoices

*Because at the higher altitude, is the higher perspective
With a higher perspective, there is Peace.*

Earth Angels have their Angel Wings

As your wings unfold you are now becoming an Angel on Earth. Embrace everyone with the unconditional love that now expands within your heart. Show compassion for those who have not yet found all their spiritual resources.

Open your wings of unconditional love fully and wrap them around the souls of those people who still need to be awake. The souls, who have yet to see. The souls, who have yet to feel. The souls who have yet to see and feel the love that they need to heal their heart.

Walk with integrity and strength. Use your wings as your tools, for helping others to realise, their full soul potential. As a worker of heart centred love you will be very blessed. There will be singing in Heaven as the Angels above rejoice.

See your own Angel Wings

Stand in front of the mirror, tall and proud
Imagine an energy enveloping you like a beautiful shroud

Then with every breath you now deeply take
See in the mirror, your unfolding wings that YOU can make!

As they spread out, and uncurl to each side, notice

their beauty
their colour and strength
through the air they swish and glide

These are your Angel Wings their presence has deep meaning
You can now soar as high as a bird; these eternal wings will help you with your healing

They wrap around you in times of need
They lift you up, to stand firmly on your feet

These Angel Wings are Heaven sent
A blessed gift!

All around you the Angels rejoice!
Another Earth Angel has made their choice
You chose Love!

Angels Wings protection for Earth Angels

As an Earth Angel your energy merges with others. The energy of love is finer and purer than the energies of greed, lust, anger and unforgiveness. People become drawn to those with fine energy, as it is healing for their soul.

Those of us who work with the Angels work with love, unconditional love. We need to protect our essence, so that we do not feel depleted. Protect yourself by wrapping yourself in the Wings of the Angels and the Archangels.

Angels enfold you in their Wings of Love

Anger is the emotion of fear. The fear of loss, abandonment, rejection, ridicule, hatred, or ignorance. Fear is the absence of Love.

Ask the Angels to be with someone who is in need of Love
Ask the Angels to enfold someone within their Wings of Love

Have compassion for yourself and others. Remember, everyone is doing the best that they can. They are doing the best that they can with the level of spiritual knowledge they currently hold in their heart, at any given time.

Anger is fear
Fear is the absence of Love

Angels are Unconditional Love
Call your Angels today

Ask the Angels to help you feel their Love
Ask the Angels to help you with your fears of loneliness, hate, anger, rejection, abandonment...
Ask the Angels to enfold you in their Wings of Love

Feel your fears dissolve in these Wings of Love
Love is the absence of fear

Where there is love
There are Angels!

Angel Wings

Here's a set of Angel wings, I'm giving them to you.
I think that you have earned them, with all the things you do.
You brighten up the days and always seem to care.
When someone needs a friend, they can always find you there.
Angel wings are rare, and given only to a few.
Reserved for Angels on Earth, Special people just like you!
By Derek Clifford

Earth Angels Walk Among Us!

The good work can now begin. We all have our part to play. The Angels walk among us. We can create Heaven on Earth.

See everything in your life from the perspective of love. Keep working with the master plan, the master plan is Unconditional Love.

We can all learn to, open our hearts and souls, more and more, little by little, day by day, moment by moment.

The rewards for love are greater than the perceived rewards of fear. The rewards of fear are illusions and can only ever be temporary in nature.

Love is the healing balm of our hearts. Each heart that heals creates healing for the planet and the Universe. Whenever you step out of the zone of love, stop! Take a breath. Say to yourself *'What is the most loving reaction I could have in this moment'?* Always come back to the moment.

The road to happiness

The road to happiness is the road with many twists and turns
The road to peace is the road with many ups and downs
The road to heaven is the road you walk with your Angels

QUESTIONS ABOUT EARTH ANGELS

I have been told that I am an Earth Angel

Hello I am new to this page, feel blessed to have found you, or my angels send me here for a reason. I'm sure will come to light in time! I'm a huge believer in angels and fairies and am told that I'm and earth angel. I've experienced many unusual events still unaware what my calling is however I don't feel I belong to this universe and there is more to my presence in this world! At times I feel out of place and from another time and place! Anyway happy to be part of this beautiful page blessings to you all.

How lovely to meet you. It really sounds to me like you are a Light worker. Light worker is another term often used for Earth Angels. You will undoubtedly have a purpose in this incarnation and it is important for your soul that you find your niche. Then you can settle into serving and your longing to go 'Home' will not be so profound and overwhelming – as your joy will come from your service. Please work with Archangel Chamuel to help to now find your Life Purpose. This will be very important for you now. Please come back to me if you have any questions on your journey. Blessings Michelle

Section 4

Preparing to meet your Angels

Purify your Home

Angels find it easier to approach you and your home where there is peace, love and harmony. All houses benefit from an Angelic purification, to remove all stale energies. These may be energies of anger, depression, lethargy, negative thoughts …. Create a peaceful haven in your home, where you can relax and open your heart and mind to the Angels.

Create an Angelic Sanctuary for your Angels

Start by opening the windows, letting in as much light and fresh air as possible. Put on some beautiful soothing music - classical music, Angel music or chanting are good examples.

- Clear away any clutter or dust
- Clean the room thoroughly with joy in your heart
- Burn some incense or use a smudge stick in each room to really transmute stuck energies
- Use Essential Oils or room sprays
- Ask the Angels of Transmutation to be with you during the whole process. Ask them to transmute lower energies in their Love and Peace. Thank the Angels and ask them to bathe all residents and visitors to your home with their angelic healing love

Carry out this purification every day for one week or until you start to feel the energies lifting. Sense the atmosphere in your home becoming finer, purer and more loving as the Angels grow closer:

- Display objects that you are drawn to, objects that create feelings of Peace; flowers, Crystals, Angel statues...
- Burn essential oils to lift the atmosphere in rooms where light or air find it difficult to circulate
- Light candles
- After an argument place a small bowl of salt in the room discreetly to absorb the negative energy vibrations (discard the next day)

- Animals like cats can help a home to feel more peaceful with their unconditional love

Finally, work on your own sense of inner peace and take some time to:

- Develop a sacred space in your life and home where you can get to know your Guardian Angel

Develop an Angelic Sacred Space

Angels love peace, harmony and love. Angels love a sacred space. It helps them to make a stronger connection to you. Create a peaceful haven within your home or office, where you can just relax and open up your heart and mind to the Angels.

Find a space where you can dedicate it to the Angels. Place items here that you are personally drawn to. These items will reflect the qualities of the Angels.

Use all the senses, creating smells, textures and energies. Use, crystals, essential oils, a small water fountain, an Angel statue, a fresh feather, candles, fresh flowers, photos or poems about Angels.

Once this sacred space is complete, light your candle or incense and then call in the Angels. Spend some quiet time just relaxing and absorbing the peaceful energies.

This is your Angel Sanctuary. Each time you sit or meditate at your sacred space ask the Angels to be with you. They will come!

I light a candle

I light a candle
I light an aromatic stick
I place my crystals

*I focus my mind
I open my heart*

*I ask for my angels to draw nearer
I see
I feel
I hear*

*I now know the presence of my Angels
Their energy
Their loving guidance
Their wisdom
Their strength
Their charity
Their Unconditional Love*

*My heart expands in gratitude
I am blessed, humbled and nurtured in my sacred space of Angelic Light
Bless You Dear Angels of the Light*

Angels and vibrational rate

Angels exist at a **higher vibrational rate or frequency. A purer state** of consciousness. When our mind is relaxed through meditation, visualisation and contemplation then our peaceful brain can now achieve the consciousness of this **higher vibrational rate. A higher vibrational rate** brings feelings of **bliss and peace.**

By raising the **vibrational rate:** there are finer and finer states of brain activity (spiritually) and greater unity with your God and the Angels. To raise your **'vibrational rate':** make a **strong connection** with **Angels** and the Angelic realms **by purifying** your environment and your life. Spend regular time in your sacred space.

Purify Yourself

An Angel is a pure being of light and exists at a higher vibrational rate or frequency. For an Angel to draw close to us, including at home and in our working environment, then we need to achieve this higher vibrational frequency or state of consciousness. We can achieve this by starting a process of purifying ourselves and purifying our home and working environments. Purification is the on-going practice of love, peace and harmony.

Develop Angelic Qualities

If you could see, touch, hear and know an Angel imagine:
- what they would look like
- their facial expression
- the way they would think and communicate
- how they would go about their day

Now start to purify yourself by developing these Angelic qualities in your own life.

How to start developing the qualities of the Angels

Every day try to work with one or more of the **angelic qualities**. The more you use angelic qualities, the more your heart will open to the Angels. They will find it easier to draw closer to you.

Try just one new quality a day and see how the positive vibration of that **angelic quality can help** you to develop a positive mind-set.

Examples of angelic qualities include:

Abundance
Acceptance
Acknowledgement
Adventure
Aspiration
Balance
Beauty
Birth
Blessings
Celebration
Compassion
Co-operation
Courage
Creativity
Curiosity
Detachment
Discernment
Discipline
Efficiency
Enthusiasm
Faith
Flexibility
Forgiveness
Freedom
Friendship
Fun
Generosity
Grace
Gratitude
Happiness
Harmony
Healing
Helpfulness
Honesty
Hope
Humour
Imagination

Inspiration
Integrity
Introspection
Intuition
Joy
Kindness
Love
Mercy
Opportunity
Patience
Peace
Playfulness
Positivity
Power
Purification
Purpose
Reliability
Responsibility
Self-worth
Serenity
Simplicity
Spontaneity
Strength
Surrender
Synchronicity
Trust
Truth
Understanding
Vulnerability
Wisdom

Angel Cards

Write each quality on a piece of cardboard to make Angel Cards. Put the cards in a small bag. Say *'Angels which quality would you like me to work on today'*? Choose one card a day to help you focus on that angelic quality.

An Angel has Loving Eyes

An Angel has a loving heart
An Angel has a divine eternal soul

An Angel protects with strength
An Angel teaches with Love

An Angel loves with compassion
An Angel speaks with integrity and non-judgement

To know the qualities of your Angel is to know the essence of your divine self
Look at your reflection in the mirror and see your own LOVING EYES!

When you look into the eyes of an Angel
You are looking into the soul of God

How to purify every aspect of your day!

1. Learn to live with simplicity

Simplicity is the path of the Angels. Allow everything in your life to flow from moment to moment. Simplicity is the key to spiritual progress.

All simple gifts like reading, walking, painting, singing, sewing, swimming, silence, these are all activities where we can just engage in the simplicity. In each moment, each sentence, each footstep, each brushstroke, every note and every stitch is the process of simplicity. In the enjoyment of simplicity we find peace. Where there is peace we find Angels.

2. In each moment choose only to see love and peace

Learn to go about your day like an Angel. Smile more and speak positively from your heart. Speak from a position of love. Only reply with comments that are loving and kind. Do not reply with hurtful or critical comments. Learn to manage your anger so that you use your energy positively. Whilst going about your day only use your energy to create love and encouragement for others. Never use your words or energy to harm others.

In every situation there is a blessing. Look at each situation from its most positive perspective. External influences can have the effect of causing us to think that we have happiness or sadness. In reality these external influences are illusions. These illusions detract you from your path of Peace.

Peace is your natural equilibrium. When you sit in stillness and you just listen to the silence, then you find within you everything that is love, contentment and joy. It is on the road of calm without the need for external gratification, that you will truly know the energy of your God and the Angels. Find your place of equilibrium and find yourself.

3. Listen with your Heart

To feel Divine Inspiration you need to open your Heart to the Angels. Angels are messengers of God. Angels speak to you through your intuition and they place feelings of love and acceptance in your heart.

In the silence, you hear Divine guidance. In the moment, you feel Divine love, with an open heart you see Divinity in everyone. Every day you can feel Divine inspiration. Ask the Angels to touch your heart. Knowing, sensing, feeling or hearing an Angel is a moment of profound love. A moment that will profoundly change your life, forever.

It is worth reaching out to an Angel today. Your requests, to know your Angels, are always heard and always granted. Angels manifest miracles for everyone.

4. Watch your thoughts, as thoughts become reality

Be aware of how you think and speak about all situations in your life. Your words and thoughts have energy and become your reality. Remember, that on-one else's words have any power to influence you. You choose your own thoughts and you choose how to receive the comments and thoughts or others. You are in control of your own life, it is not in control of you.

5. Heal your Heart

Learn how to master your emotions through the process of detachment and forgiveness. Learn how to ask your Angels for emotional healing.
Detachment - Practice detachment; let others live their lives while you live yours. Do not label situations as good or bad. A situation just 'is'!
Forgiveness - Learn to forgive yourself and others and to see the good in everyone despite seeming appearances. Forgiveness does not mean that what has happened to you, or what someone has done to you, is

acceptable. Forgiveness means that you will no longer allow that situation or behaviour to hurt or affect you.

6. Learn the art of clarity

Focus on your hearts desires and gain clarity as to how you will feel when they manifest. Fill your mind with positive mantras and affirmations. Learn to be calm and patient, and to accept that everything has its own divine timing and synchronicity.

Detach from the need to have material possessions and know that all that we need is provided at exactly the right time that we need it. Watch for the signs and synchronicities that will be sent to help you during each and every stage of your journey.

7. Act with integrity

Be strong, act as a warrior of Light. You are responsible for everything that does or does not occur in your life. Always speak with truth, honesty and integrity. Avoid people, situations or places that do not resonate with the qualities of peace or love.

8. Be content, show Gratitude

Go through each day with a smile in your heart. Create fun and laughter. Go about your daily chores with love in your heart, ask the Angels to join you. Make every step of your life a life with the Angels, invite them in. Ask them to help you and be with you every day.

9. Be generous

Learn to give generously from your heart of love. Give as you would wish to receive. Always listen to the perspective of another from your heart.

10. Enjoy your Angels

Flow through your day effortlessly and easily as you learn to call an Angel each day to be with you. Call your Angels to surround you during your sleep so that you rest peacefully and rise refreshed and positive. Sing to your Angels, read about Angels, write to your Angels. Fill your life with love, laughter, peace and joy.

11. Inner Child

Become comfortable with your inner child through healing and meditation.

12. Earth Angel

Work with the qualities of the Earth Angels to transform your life and the life of others around you.

Summary

We can ask the Angels to help us purify our lives. By purifying our life we can help our souls to be awakened and filled with the Light and qualities of the Angels.

To practice purity in our lives then we must first imagine how the Angels go about their day:

- what they look like – their facial expressions
- how they feel and think
- how they go about their day

Imagine that one day you can also be enlightened like an Angel

- take up some voluntary work
- learn to manage your anger – take a deep breath and count to 10
- do not reply to people with hurtful or critical comments
- in every moment try to see love and peace
- It is important to purify yourself and simplify your life. Love is always the answer!

Deeper Personal Purification

Release Ego - Love is always the answer

Thank your Angels for showing you that love is always the answer. Heal your Ego.

Ego is Fear? Love is always the answer as Ego is indeed fear. **However,** in the realms of the Earthly dimensions, **ego is indeed necessary. It is necessary** to drive us and to maintain our motivation

Without ego we would be pure forms of energy, unconditional love. We would float around with nothing to compare ourselves against. There would be no evolution or expansion of the Universe. We would have no ability to use our sense. It is through using our senses that our souls are able to grow. When we decided to incarnate we chose this egoic state so that our **souls could experience all the senses.**

Ego is necessary to drive our lives forward. It is a positive trait **when used in conjunction** with a **loving open heart. A loving open heart,** that wants to grow through service.

Any activity carried out by the **ego for self-gratification is fear. Fear and love cannot exist in the same space.** You can only be **one or the other in any moment.**

Our ego helps us to **monitor which direction we are going in** and helps us to maintain whatever journey we choose.

Ask the Angels to help you **walk in the direction of Love. U**se the impetus of **Self-Love *'for the higher good of all concerned'*** as your motivation. **We are all interconnected.** Your Love is my Love, my love is your Love. **Love** the symbiotic nourishment for **the evolution of humanity.**

Heal the hurt in your Soul

The Soul is your individual beacon of Light. It can never be extinguished. However, over life-times, layers become encased around the Soul. This occurs;

- through negative beliefs and programming
- through the accumulation of Karma
- through unresolved life lessons and initiations

Ask your Angels today, to draw close to you
Ask them to gently start to peel back the layers, blocking the light of your Soul
Ask them to help you release Karma
Ask them to help you release programming and negative patterns
Ask them to guide you through your life lessons so that this time you can complete them and move forward.

As each of the layers of negative energies, beliefs, programming, karma and life lessons are gently peeled back, then the Soul receives more Divine Light. It starts to Heal.

The Soul starts to once again be awake!
The Light from your Angels will feed your Soul, its Light expanding it more and more. The love and light from your Angels will start to heal every recess, memory and miasm in your entire holistic being.

See the Oneness

Your healing, will create Peace in your Soul. This Peace will touch others and their process of removing layers can then also begin.

We are all interconnected
We are all beacons of Soul Light
We can all heal together

We are all One. We are all interconnected

Heal your Inner Child

The **Inner Child** is the part of our energetic make-up that has been programmed by external influences.

During this and many previous lifetimes;

the **events** in our lives
the **teachings** in our lives
the **parents** in our lives
the **government** in our lives

are all **external forces** which contribute to the **awareness of our inner child**. The inner child is the part of us that reacts subconsciously to outward stimuli. This outward stimuli at a subconscious level has:

formed repeating patterns
syndromes
depression
anger
happiness, joy, excitement, anticipation. These are all the **reactions of the inner child to external influences**

Where the **inner child** is afraid, then working with your **Angels** can help to nurture and heal you, creating self-esteem and good health.

Where the **inner child** is confident, secure and loved, then working with the **Angels** can help you use your inner qualities to help others.

In reality we all have an aspect of a **frightened inner child** and a **confident inner child.** Working with the **Angels** can help you to **balance** the two. **Where there is balance there is a healing.**

Angels heal
Angels guide
Angels nurture

Angels help us to come into balance

To heal and balance your **inner child** call your **Guardian Angel** to your side
Ask your **Guardian Angel** to help you release any imbalances today!

Angels Embrace the Meek and Mild

Angels embrace the meek and mild, mending broken wings
Angels help you to lift up your emotions and to find your inner child

When you have faith, belief, and trust, then an Angel is always by your side, nurturing your soul. This Angels is always boldly leading you through your life, showing you all the gifts of joy, protection and hope.

With the love of an Angel, your life becomes visible from a different and higher perspective. The layers within your heart begin to peel back and your *soul essence* shines through. Only a healed heart can be the final result of embracing Divine love.

Angels embrace the meek and mild
Glory be to God and his Angelic team

Love is like a seed

Love is like a seed in everyone's hearts
To flourish and grow it needs to trust. It needs to feel the light of God and the Angels
Open your heart to the light and miracles will unfold

Ask the Angels to help you feel the Light
Ask the Angels to help you feel the Love

As you feel it, so must you send it to others. For it is in the sharing of love that everything is healed.

Love heals war giving peace
Love heals pain giving healing
Love heals despair giving hope and faith

Love equals new beginnings

In each and every moment choose love for yourself and others. Send it as a beacon of light from the centre of your heart to Everyone and Everything!

Send to those who need hope, peace, faith, and healing today!

The Angels will bless those who use their love to heal others
The Angels will bless those who use their love to heal themselves

Where there is unconditional love a healing must always occur, it is Divine Law.

Where there is Unconditional Love
There are Angels!

Love is given to us as a Gift

We are all keepers of a Pure Heart and the light of Love ignites within us unconditional love.
Love is accessible from your God, through the angelic interactions we have each and every moment. Angels are messengers of God and are made of divine essence.

By inviting the Angels into your life, you will experience this gift of love. You will feel it as it floods your pure heart.

Allow it to bathe you
To heal you
To protect you
To nurture you

Allow your pure heart to swell with this unconditional love. Allow it to flow out, greeting other people that you meet.

We all have access to a pure heart
We all have access to the Angels

We all have access to unconditional love
We can all learn to embrace others with our pure heart of love

---

The mirror of your Soul

Go to the mirror
Look at your soul
Is it happy, healed full of Love?

Your eyes will tell you the answer

Heal yourself with the Love of your Angels
Look into the eyes of your Angel
The eyes of your Angel will beam out loving healing light from its soul

See it, feel it, absorb it, drink it in

Go to the Mirror
You will now have the Love you need to see

Meditation to heal the Inner Child

Preparation

- Breathe slowly in and out until you feel completely relaxed
- Imagine that you have roots growing from your feet into the centre of the earth
- Continue until you feel grounded

White Light

- White light enters your crown and is now filling your entire body
- As you breathe in keep bringing in more and more white light
- As you breathe out imagine the white light going out of your mouth to form a white bubble of protection all around you

Calling in your 'Guardian Angel'

Call in your **Guardian Angel,** feel her loving energy around you, like loving mother energy.

Open your heart to your **Guardian Angel** and feel her loving energy sweeping and swirling away any hurt. Allow your Guardian Angel to heal your heart, deep into your past.

Feel your heart opening more and more. Allow in more and more healing and nurturing light

Healing your 'inner child'

See yourself sitting inside your own heart, allow the white light to smooth and soothe you.
Your **Guardian Angel** is handing you a baby, a pure white baby. This is your **inner child.**

Love and nurture this child. Tell your **inner child** how much you love it unconditionally.
Feel the light of the **Guardian Angel** healing you and your **inner child.**

Finishing the meditation

When you have finished speaking to your **inner child,** thank your **Guardian Angel.**
Return to the room, and open your eyes

You can go back at any time to heal and meet your **inner child**
Visit your heart with your **Guardian Angel** often. Each visit will help to create a stronger and deeper healing.

Angelic Journal

Write down your experiences in your Angel journal
Go for a walk in nature to help you to ground this experience

The Aura – your protective coat

The aura is our protective coat. It helps us to grow spiritually; it helps us to keep healthy. The colour spectrums displayed in our aura draws to our side Angelic help.

To strengthen your aura, purify your life, purify your mind, purify your environment.
Take a walk in nature
Think positively about yourself and others
Be grateful for everything you do have
Give as you would like to receive
Know that, whatever the seeming illusions, the Angels walk with you

A strong aura, creates a stronger connection to the Angelic realms

Rainbow of Peace – the Aura

An aura is the energetic and magnetic field around your body, which is normally invisible to the untrained eye.

Your aura provides protection for your physical body and holds information. It holds information in the form of energies which are both coming into your energetic space or going out of your energetic space.

All negative thoughts and traumas gather as miasms or blockages in the different levels of your aura. If you don't heal your aura this can create imbalances in your health. It can create imbalances in your holistic being emotionally, physically, psychologically and spiritually. In order to keep the aura healthy and strong, then you need to learn about your entire energy system, which includes the 'chakras'.

Your aura is constantly changing based on your conscious and subconscious energy. It acts as a beacon to the Universe.

During meditation and visualisation you can ask that any holes, blockages or miasms in your aura be healed.

Imagine your aura being purified by the light and love of the Angels. Imagine it cleansing and rebalancing every part of your aura from your past and present. Imagine the healing light and love entering every cell, liquid and organ within your body.

By taking time to work with the energy field of your aura, you can be healed on many levels. The aura is your holistic development tool. The colours of the aura at any time are not as important as the overall health of the aura at any given moment.

To make your aura healthy balance all your chakras regularly, so that their colours radiate vibrantly. A healthy chakra system will emit all the colours of the rainbow.

How to see an aura – your protective coat

To see your own aura close your eyes

Imagine yourself sitting in a chair in front of you
Imagine you are looking at your identical self

In meditative and calm state, look at the aura around your identical self and start work imagine the aura around you.

As you breathe in, imagine golden light entering through the feet of your identical self, filling its entire body

As you breathe out, imagine golden light entering through the crown of your identical self, filling its entire auric space

Imagine the outward breath of your identical self, breathing the golden energy out to form a protective bubble. Each breath makes the aura stronger and healthier. See this clearly around your identical self. Now imagine this spiritual coat also surrounds and protects you. The luminosity of this golden aura is now visible to the Angels. The Angels will now be drawn to you.

Your Golden Aura

Pave the way ahead with Gold
Not the Gold of money, but the Gold of enlightenment

Your Golden Aura ....
becomes your colour for Wisdom
becomes your colour for Grace
becomes your colour for Unconditional Love, Peace... Joy
Gold the colour of Angels

Breath in the colour of Gold
Breath in the colour of Angels

You are building a rainbow

As you progress along your spiritual path you will be presented with tasks or initiations. Some will be harder to master than others. Some may come again and again. The harder the task the bigger the reward.

You will never be asked to undertake a task which:

Was not agreed prior to your incarnation
Is more than your soul can bear
You will never be given a task that you are not worthy of completing

With each initiation you are awarded a colour for your aura. One by one, lifetime by lifetime, you are building a rainbow. This rainbow becomes the bridge from your Soul to Heaven.

When you walk with your Angels, you can call out to them when a ravine appears on your path. You need to complete the task, you have seen this one before, but somehow it returns and just gets more difficult. Difficulty is a sign of spiritual progress.

Remember, one step at a time. Dig deep for your strength and with integrity and honesty, tell the Angels everything:

All your fears
All your doubts

Ask that this time you can complete the task and reach new levels of peace and joy. Continue with the task. Step by step, moment by moment. Be confident and know that whilst the ridge may seem steep and narrow, your Angelic Team will not let you fall.

After you have crossed the ravine you will now step on to the fresh new terrain. Your energy and vibration will now be more finely attuned.

Changes recently made to your energy pattern can stir up sudden volatility. It can stir up unsettling situations, especially with people around you. This is a sign that you are changing. The external reaction is a sign that the remnants of stuck energies are now being healed and released.

As you change your energy frequency, it is like changing a radio station. At first everything seems different and not quite what you are used to, the switching between channels is fuzzy and distorted. You can't quite comprehend your new position clearly.

The new frequency arrives more strongly as you continue to adjust and monitor your internal controls. Once the new station/frequency kicks in, everything is clearer, more focused and smooth. You can now move forward confidently.

Your new vibration is beaming out loud and clear for others to enjoy. Any anger has now shifted to another frequency, but you now vibrate at the frequency of peace and joy. As the signal becomes even stronger, then any occasional blips are quickly realigned. You resume your new vibration of peace and joy. Peace is now your normal emotional level from moment to moment.

Finding peace and releasing anger is a major tool of learning in our lives. Once anger is addressed and replaced with confidence, assertiveness and honesty then peace will prevail and a major spiritual initiation has been completed.

Chakras – Spiritual wheels of Energy

Chakras are spiritual wheels of energy that can be seen and felt by intuitives. Their purpose is to hold all your spiritual knowledge in perfect alignment for your spiritual growth.
When your chakras are perfectly aligned and balanced, then the next level of spiritual understanding will be bestowed upon you. The chakras can accelerate your spiritual journey when they are flowing freely with no blockages or imbalances.

Chakras are wheels of energy which spin at different frequencies and speeds within your auric field. Chakra imbalances can lead to the manifestation of illnesses and disease. Learn about each Chakra and its different role in your energy system. Each chakra will need to be regularly cleansed, purified and aligned, in order to create balance.

The chakra system is 'holistic' and when it is in perfect alignment you have homeostasis. This is where you are in balance physically, emotionally, psychologically and spiritually. The balancing of the chakras provides a perfect barometer for you to assess all aspects of your life. The balance you achieve in your chakra system will be reflected in your health and current life story.

Chakras are influenced by your:
emotions
past life programming
beliefs
thoughts
environment
the food you eat, what you drink
how you feel

Archangels and Chakras

Each chakra is overseen by an Archangel. Call upon the Archangels and visualise them bathing, nurturing and re-aligning each chakra. Imagine each chakra whizzing and whirling at the perfect vibration and resonance for you.

Base Chakra – Archangel Gabriel
Sacral Chakra – Archangel Gabriel
Solar Plexus – Archangel Uriel
Heart Chakra – Archangel Chamuel
Throat Chakra – Archangel Michael
Third Eye Chakra – Archangel Raphael
Crown Chakra – Archangel Jophiel

Learn about its corresponding Archangel
Learn to feel the energy of each chakra individually
Learn to balance your chakra system regularly

Ask your Angels to help you. Feel the peace, as your life becomes more balanced, non-attached to outcomes, and flowing. This is the sign of a chakra system in perfect balance.
Write everything in your Angel Journal.

Namaste: *'The peace and love in me, recognises the peace and love in you'*

Chakras and Auras work together.....

The chakras and the aura work together symbiotically. Each one supporting the other. The chakra colours flow out into the aura creating a swirling pattern of colours based on your level of spiritual emotional and psychological development.

The Chakras emit different colours as you expand and develop your levels of spiritual consciousness. For example, an unawakened base chakra may emit Red if it is in balance. A base chakra that is awakened and is spiritually developed will gradually change move into the colour of platinum.

How can I balance my Aura and my Chakras?

Meditation every day is important. Regular meditation on your chakras and your aura creates balance and alignment.

Regular meditation has many benefits because your:

chakra system becomes stronger
health becomes more vibrant
clarity becomes more focused

Your refreshed aura will create an energetic field which will attract more Angel light. Ask the Angels today to help you relax quickly and effortlessly, so that you can meditate daily and clear and balance your chakras. When you have perfect alignment you have homeostasis - balance.

Where there are balanced and healthy chakras
There are Angels!

Chakra and Aura healing with the Angels

Preparation

Lie comfortably
Play some soothing music, like Angel music, classical music.....
Light some incense and a candle to enhance the vibration of the room

Call in the Angels

Rub your hands together briskly. Now imagine the Angels streaming healing light through your body, starting from your head.

Imagine the light coming into your body through your crown chakra right down to the tips of your fingers. As the light enters your crown chakra you may feel a slight tingling or warmth.

As it reaches your fingertips, place your hands over your Crown (Chakra 1) at the top of your head. Feel the energy as it moves through and onto each and every chakra in order:

Crown chakra
Third eye chakra
Throat chakra
Heart chakra
Solar plexus chakra
Sacral Chakra
Base Chakra

Focus on each chakra for as long as feels necessary, before moving onto the next. Learn to feel the different energies, feelings and sensations as you move between them.

Once your chakras have been replenished use any additional crystalline white light to fill your aura. The aura is your protective spiritual coat which sits around your body.

Thank the Angels. Write down any experiences in your Angel Journal .

QUESTIONS ABOUT AURAS AND CHAKRAS

I am just exhausted of the path I have been on (lost)…

Michelle thank you for responding…. At the risk of sounding petty.. I am just exhausted of the path I have been on … (lost) I am not sure of anything in respect of where I am going in life.. and why is it no matter how different I try to be in choosing the men in my life…. I get the same result from them ugh!

When we are not sure where we are going, this is a good sign. It is a good sign because we are becoming more aware and focused about our life plan and its connection to our spirituality.

Archangel Gabriel can help us when we need to reassess exactly where we are up to, how far we have come. Archangel Gabriel can help us to decide in which direction we will take our next step. Archangel Gabriel's nurturing pure and radiant white light of purification will help you to put your life plan into perspective.

The spiritual path can be arduous and exhausting and this is why spiritual seekers will be so highly rewarded as they reach the pinnacle of their quest.

Again, exhaustion is only a positive sign of how hard you have been transforming, healing and regenerating at a soul level. These realignments cause your entire body mass, mind and soul to radiate and vibrate more finely and more peacefully. When we radiate peace, we are radiating peace for all.

As your vibration becomes finer and purer, then heavy situations like anger, depression, hostility can be exhausting for you. Your now finely vibrating aura mops up all this negativity like a sponge. Your aura of love heals everything unlike itself. Your aura is constantly working and as such you are valued with the label of Light worker or Earth Angel.

- Take some time to become re-balanced when you start to feel exhausted emotionally, physically, psychologically, and spiritually
- Take time to meditate on all your chakras, clearing them, balancing them, realigning them. The health of your chakras affects the health of your aura and it is important to keep your aura vibrant and healthy

With some spiritual time set aside just for you, meditate and speak to your Angels in exactly the same way as you have written your thoughts to me today. You can walk in nature, you can set your goals and you can purify and rebalance. These feelings of exhaustion and uncertainty will then subside.

Concentrate on this moment, don't worry about how things will unfold. You have done the hardest part of your task now and soon you will reach a 'plateau of peace'. When you breathe in the fresh new air, from this new perspective, you will smile. You will look down and you will see how far you have come.

Relationships with others during these times of change will also be tools for learning. Take this time to rebalance and really think and visualise in your heart, how it would feel to meet your Divine Love. Then go about each moment refining all the qualities you seek, from a mate, inside of yourself.

Ask your Angels to be with you every step of the way. They will help you to assimilate all changes in your life smoothly. Ask them to help you to have the energy to see how far you have come. Your focus will now be on enjoying each and every moment. Write everything in your Angelic Journal. Let me know how you get along. Blessings Michelle

Grounding

What does grounded mean? **Grounded** means that your energies are firmly aligned inside your body and in line with your chakra system. To be ungrounded can create temporary chaos, confusion even illusion. It can create vertigo and flu-like symptoms for a short period of time.

To be **grounded** walk tall with your **head and heart in heaven**, but with your **feet firmly planted on the ground.** It is easier to manifest your **hearts desires** when you are **grounded**, because you have **focus, clarity, and clear intention.** Your **hearts desires** become firmly rooted into the ground like seedlings, **when you are grounded. A**t the **correct time** they will **manifest** into your **hearts desires**

Ask the **Angels** to help you stay **grounded** and **protected** throughout your day
Stay in the moment and concentrate on your **breath**
Place your feet firmly on the floor or if lying imagine your feet are firmly on the floor
Imagine that below you is soft green grass and soft warm earth

From your feet imagine that tiny roots are growing into the earth as if you were a tree
Imagine the roots growing bigger and stronger, and going deeper and deeper
When the roots reach the centre of the Earth, they find a crystal
Let the roots wrap firmly around the crystal

Bring any wisdom from the crystal back up the roots into your feet and then up into your entire body. You are now grounded and can move onto your meditation with your Angel.

My daughter sees Angels, but is now getting nasty visions

My daughter is getting nasty visions she has mental illness the angels haven't been to visit her lately she say xx

In the eyes of God and the Angels your daughter is perfect. Imagine her perfection and without doubt bathe her with loving thoughts of her perfection. Keep these thoughts and feelings of perfection of your Heart.

Your heartfelt Love and thoughts will absorb into your environment, this will help her to be free of lower energies and help her to heal. When doubts come in, go into meditation, in your sacred space and ask the Angels to help you to feel thoughts of your daughter in her perfection. The perfection as seen by the eyes of God. Allow it to fill your heart.

When your heart is full imagine this loving energy beaming out like a shower of light all over your daughter and your home. Ask that the Angels love, protect and heal you both on all levels, for the highest good of all concerned.

Do this meditation often.
Spray Rose scented spray around your home, to encourage the Angels to draw close
Know that the Angels now reside there with you both, you can now release all your fears, and anxieties to be taken by the Angels to the heart of God.
Thank them
Write everything in your Angelic Journal

So many changes, I have a concern about my altar? - Submitted by Community Member

good morning Michelle and Angels - a question or concern of mine about altars - this past year has been quite the process of change in so many literal senses - due to unstable place to live - finding self-knowing where geographically feel better and have not been able to return due to 'felt responsibilities' -

i have been moving too much -ego maybe? but also my private/personal area was, i feel 'invaded' resulting in feelings of negativity and violation - chasing assistance and time escaping even though All in divine timing-

but as humans can only take so much but heart drawn to soul - as the life shifts, so has mind- my 'altar' has shifted, changed, unsure if rightly done to begin with - but now have some items packed - wanting or needing confirmation that they know the good intent and that the courage i need to fulfil 'my' part during this process of closing some doors so that i may re-enter the open windows of opportunities of love ahead that i know are patiently waiting but getting tired...

in gratitude for much - thank you for being a teacher messenger...- have a good day xo

Hello, your moving around is due to your energy field changing its vibration as you process and purify at deeper and deeper levels. With this deep purification you vibrate finer and purer. As such, the environment where you are based is no longer a match. During times of intense changes as you say, then you may find yourself moving frequently and the things in and around you may also keep changing.

None of this is anything to worry about, as it is a sign that you are healing the lower aspects of your ego. In the past this the lower aspects of your ego would of kept you attached to things, people and possessions that may of been holding you back.

It has all been leading you to your spiritual home or geographical area. This is important because your purified being will now be placed in exactly the correct location to help raise the energy of the planet. This is part of a process for the whole of humanity, and you are part of an awesome team who is undertaking the process of purification and Ascension in order to assist.

The Angels will have been with you during all these challenging changes and will now be helping you to keep calm and centred. All the pieces are being moved into place. We are all interconnected. We are all One!

Just BE in your PEACE now Dear One. Many Blessings will be sent to you for your part in the Divine Plan. You have chosen at a soul level to work in service for the benefit of the masses. This will still continue, but you will now be in your BLISS and a space of equilibrium.

All intent comes from your Heart, not from the possessions around you. Just Bless those objects that you like and that help you to feel Peace. With this loving intention they will also carry the vibration of Peace. Your Angels say to you that your soul work does not go unnoticed. Blessings as always for your lovely question.... Michelle

Section 5

How to connect with your Angels

How to connect with your Angels

There are various ways we can call upon and connect with our Angels. To connect with Angels then we need to learn to work with all our senses. When we develop all our senses then we become ever more skilled in seeing, sensing and knowing. We become more sensitive to what is going on around us, moment by moment.

To connect with our Angels it is important for us to start an inner journey of relaxation and contemplation. As we become more peaceful in our mind and soul, we are then able to hear and see more clearly the Angelic signs that are being sent to us regularly.

There are many ways to start releasing your inner chatter. By releasing your inner chatter you can then just focus on the one sound that is important. That sound is the sound of your intuition speaking to you through the feelings in your Heart.

Angels speak to us through the intuition and feelings in our Heart.

Today is the first day of the rest of your life

Today is the first day of the rest of your life. What will you do to change your life for the better? Will you walk aimlessly through each moment, not seeing, not hearing, not feeling? Will you show no awareness for the wonder of the miracle of life around you? The wonder of evolution, of our Universe of your God? Will you continue to walk in a world of one dimension, with greed, with anger, hatred, lust?

Just within a thought is something more magnificent. It is within your grasp. But with this lack of awareness your Angels sit aimlessly without any task. They are just waiting for you to ask them for their help and assistance. Ask the Angels to be with your now. Say *'I am just one step away from knowing a different way of life'*.

Embrace everything around you with all your senses. Start to train your mind for more peace and more awareness:

Really see things – see the details
Really smell things – smell the aroma
Really hear things – hear the Universe
Really feel things – feel the richness of touch
Really taste things – enjoy the taste of your favourite food, savour it

Develop all these 5 senses. These 5 senses help you to know implicitly that there is something greater than self. You will start to experience the *awakening*. Today is the first day of the rest of your life.

Hearing Angelic Inspiration - Awakening

To hear Divine Inspiration then you need to open your heart to the Angels. Angels are your personal messengers between Heaven and Earth. Angels speak to you through your intuition, through the feelings of love and acceptance in your Heart. When you silence your mind you hear Divine Guidance. In that moment you feel Divine Love. With your open heart you see Divinity in everyone and everything... you are inspired. Feel your Divine Inspiration today, as the Angels help you to open your Heart.

Knowing, sensing, feeling or hearing an Angel is a moment of profound Love. A moment that changes your life It is a moment of Divine Inspiration.

Where there is LOVE, there are ANGELS!

Love begins in a moment, a moment of truth, a moment of realisation. Love grows in a moment of peace, stillness and calm creating a connection with the Divine Essence.

In the presence of Love
Your Heart can feel

Your Heart can speak
And your Heart can mend

The Way forward is to be in your peace
The way forward is to ask the Angels to embrace you in their stillness and Love
The way forward is through the Angel's loving vibrations and Love Divine

Once you have felt this power within you, then you can produce this feeling of security and peace for another.

Everything starts in a moment. Let your moment be NOW!
An open Heart is a loving Heart.

Where there is love
There are ANGELS!

Everything starts in a moment. Let your moment be NOW!

Meditation-Peace training for the mind

What is Meditation?

Meditation is *'peace training'* for the mind. Meditation is the focusing of your thoughts, on one object, one subject or your breath. These methods help us to create more clarity, focus and peace.

Meditation is a tool for spiritual development and helps you to engage with your Angels or to embark on your spiritual journey. Once on the spiritual path, meditation can propel you to a higher level of self-awareness, thus helping you with your spiritual progression.

Meditation is best practised regularly, initially for short periods of time. As you train your mind to focus, then the process of meditation will become easier and become a mode for relaxation.

Why do I need to meditate?

Normally our minds are full of chatter and distractions. We have anxieties, lists, emotions, problems, deadlines, aches and pains. When we first sit down to practice meditation all these distractions become apparent.

In Buddhism this distraction of the mind is referred to as the *'monkey-mind'*. The monkey mind dances around, back and forth. However, through continued practice, then meditation will become a training of peace. A training of peace for your mind. It will teach the mind how to only focus on one thing. Whilst you are focusing on that one thing, your mind cannot focus on anything else. For example: you may focus on the feeling of love in your heart.

With regular practice meditation will become easier and easier. At first, you will only be able to concentrate in short bursts, maybe only seconds. But by gently bringing your focus back, again and again and again!, your mind will gradually be able to concentrate for longer and longer. Meditation is all the spurts of focus melded together into a steady flow.

What are the benefits of Meditation?

- Stress Reduction
- Resilience and skills to manage stress
- Ability to focus on the now
- Peaceful mind – less negative emotions

Meditation and illness

Meditation may be helpful for conditions where stress is a precipitating factor:
- Allergies
- Anxiety Disorders
- Asthma
- Binge eating

- Cancer
- Depression
- Fatigue
- Heart Disease
- High Blood Pressure
- Pain
- Sleep Problems
- Substance Abuse ……

Meditation is the route to meeting your Angels

Meditation is the route to peace. By focusing your mind, you teach your thoughts to become calm. With small regular sessions your mood will lift, the seeming frustrations of your life will no longer hold significance; you will open to the wisdom of non-attachment.

When you are no longer attached to outcomes or to controlling outcomes, you are free! When you have freedom, you have peace. Angels are drawn to the feelings of peace.

What greater gift to give another than your feeling of inner peace
When we all have peace, the world will be healed

Meditation is peace training for the mind. As our thoughts reduce to a much slower pace, the brain waves change. By slowing the frequency we create a vibration of peace and calmness and this creates a resonance with the vibration of Angels.

The Light of the Angels which is fine and pure, can now easily access your physical space. The mind having slowed to a different pace is now in a state similar to when we have deep refreshing sleep. During deep refreshing sleep the body can heal.

During your meditation your thoughts of peace and calm accelerate your natural healing mechanism, and you draw in the healing essence of your Angels.

Meditation - the route to Enlightenment

As our thoughts reduce to a much slower pace, our brain waves change. By slowing the frequency, we create a vibration of peace and calmness. This peace and calmness resonates with the vibration of Angels.

The Angels can now approach you and their healing waves and sonics merge into your being. You are becoming at one with the love of the Angels. Continued and regular practice allows this process of merging with the love of the Angels and it takes you on a journey towards Enlightenment.

Enlightenment is a profound moment where you see the world through different eyes.
You see the world from a different perspective, you realise there is no separation. You realise that everything is in fact, One.

Once the seed of Enlightenment has been planted, then true Peace and Love for all is understood at a soul level. Your whole perspective changes to *'How may I serve'?* You realise that your service affects the whole.

Meditation, visualisation, contemplation. These are all essential tools for training the mind for Peace.

It is in the silence that we hear

Guardian Angel Meditation

Find regular time to just be calm and peaceful. Take time to learn about the presence of your Angels. When you think about your Angels that is a sign that your Angel is with you.

Meditation with your Angel

Meditation undertaken in a dedicated space or room, at a regular time will help your mind and senses to quickly acquire the skills of peace, serenity and tranquillity.

Meditation Essentials

- Your meditation room should be comfortably warm and clean of clutter
- Open a window slightly
- Choose a regular time to practise meditation – dawn or dusk are most effective
- Make sure you will not be disturbed for at least 30 minutes
- Make a simple altar as a focus point
- Make yourself comfortable with pillows, rugs and cushions
- Have an extra layer of clothing or a blanket to cover yourself as your temperature may drop during meditation

Meditation Preparation

- Light a candle and /or incense
- Play some soothing Angelic or relaxing music
- Use essential oils in a burner, or a room spray
- Place fresh flowers in your meditation room
- Take a shower or bath and put on clean clothes before you begin
- Wear loose comfortable clothing preferably pastel colours or white
- Hold a crystal

Meditation Posture

- Sit cross-legged or in the lotus yoga position on the floor
- Put a cushion under you so that your pelvis is tilted slightly forward
- Keep your back straight but relaxed
- If your prefer to sit in a chair then choose a straight backed chair and make sure your feet are flat on the floor
- Rest your palms upwards in your lap or rest your palms down on your knees
- If you prefer you can lie flat in the sleep posture

Grounding

- Once you are comfortable imagine that you have roots growing out of the soles of your feet
- Imagine these roots growing deeply and firmly into the earth below you until they reach the centre of the earth

- If you are seated, you can also imagine additional roots growing from the base of your spine into the earth

Relax

- Now take some time to focus on your breathing
- Breathe in to the word love
- Breathe out to the word peace
- In love, out peace
- Continue in a pattern that is comfortable for you until you start to feel relaxed
- Just allow any passing thoughts to come and go

Bring down the essence of your Angel

- Once you are relaxed imagine the essence of your Angels entering into your body through your head
- Imagine this essence as a bright golden light, going right down to your feet and out through the roots to the earth
- Allow the Angel Essence and Light to fill you, every organ, every cell, every thought
- As you breathe in more Angel Essence enters your body
- As you breathe out - breathe out Peace
- Imagine the Peace forming a bubble of protection all around your body, you are totally relaxed and safe in your bubble of peace
- This peace is the peace from your Angel, you are now connected
- Allow the meditation to naturally flow

Finish the meditation

- Thank your Angels
- Open your eyes
- Write down everything that you experienced today in your Angelic Journal

Be like a Cat with peace in the moment – Mindfulness Meditation

How often have you eaten a meal and never really tasted it? Many things pass us during our day but our minds are always somewhere else and distracted.

To find peace and inner happiness then one useful tool is to learn how to be in the moment, a moment of mindfulness.

Mindfulness is being aware of your actions, your thoughts and your senses. It is not possible to live in the moment all the time, but with practice you can learn to live in the moment for longer and longer. This gives you a sense of stress relief and quality of life.

There will always be times when you find yourself thinking about the future or the past, but with training you can bring your thoughts back to the moment, more quickly and more easily each time.

Here are five examples to help you:

1. *Children* – There's no one better than being in the present than a child. To be childlike is to experience the world in the moment. You see things and experience things for the first time. You are in a state of wonder and awe.
2. *Cats and Animals live in the moment* - They only think about sleeping, running, eating, loving unconditionally, Being. Animals are perfect examples of living in the moment.
3. *Eating Chocolate* - When we really enjoy eating something we savour every mouthful. Be in the moment; eat everything as if it were your favourite food. Savour the flavour, the temperature, how it melts in your mouth, how it makes you feel.
4. *Ironing or Washing Up* - Whilst Ironing or washing the dishes, try to concentrate on every aspect of the job in hand. The water

flowing from the tap, the bubbles in the soap, the sound, the warmth on your hands, the tinkling of the cutlery, the sound of the iron as it steams away the creases. Use each sensation to draw you back to the moment.
5. *Be absorbed* in something you enjoy. Gardening, Painting, Sewing. When you are absorbed in something, you are in the moment. You are lost in the task and not distracted by your thoughts. You are fully concentrating on the task in hand.

Being in the moment is the path to Peace. Ask the Angels to help you release any negative or repeating mind-sets, patterns, thoughts, feelings, situations in your life that do not allow you to live in the present moment.

Be in the moment, be peaceful like a cat!

Questions on meditation

Can the Angels reach us in a noisy house?

I really never have the chance to meditate. My home is never quiet. Does this mean that Angels can't come to me?

Dear One, Peace is a place in your heart, which can never be erased or drowned out by any external situation or noise. Peace is a process. A process where in each moment you come back to the now!

Mindfulness is a form of meditation. Where you focus on something. You focus on that thing as you are doing it. In the focus of that activity your mind becomes calmer and quieter. For example: When you are preparing the dinner, you prepare the vegetables. One vegetable at a time, One slice at a time, One moment at a time.

Focus on the vegetable. How does it feel, how does it smell. What colour is it. What size is it? How healthy is it? Really focus on this vegetable as the cool water washes it, watch how the water drains away. As you are noticing all the details say to yourself *"I am in the moment, I am at Peace'*, *'I am in the moment, I am at Peace'*. Do this exercise with anything and everything. When your child is screaming *' I am in the moment. I am at Peace'*

Make your life a living meditation. Keep coming back to the details, the feelings, the tastes, the sounds. A noisy home is a peaceful home when everyone is enjoying and focusing on the moment. Say to your children *'One thing at a time'*. Angels love happy homes with the noise of happy families.

Ask the Angels to help you see, feel and know them in every aspect of your life and your home. The peace is on the inside, inside your Heart and Soul Dear One.

Where there is Peace
There are Angels

Is meditation –false Gods?

Is meditation not the worship of false Gods?

Meditation is peace training for the mind. It is a process of changing the thoughts and patterns within your mind, so that you are more able, to clearly hear the voice of your soul.

In hearing your soul, it will guide you to the best resources to help you with the purpose of your life. The purpose of your life is to heal through your service.

Nothing can interfere with a calm, peaceful mind. It is the one most important tool for strength on all levels. It is the one biggest tool for helping you to accelerate your spiritual path or awaken to it.

During meditation, the ego is trained to step aside. Ego is fear. With the ego to one side, your only input will now be Love.

There can be no false prophets in the space called Love. Love and Fear cannot exist in the same place at the same time.

Meditate on Love
Call in the Angels of Love
Breathe in Love
Breathe out Love
Now relax and listen to your heart as a journey begins to unfold

Any journey guided by Angels and the heart, will be a journey of Love and Peace. Meditation is peace training for the mind. A peaceful mind equals a peaceful Heart.

Where there is a peaceful Heart, there are Angels
Where there are Angels, there is Love

Angelic Journal

During your journey with the Angels it is important to write everything in your Angel journal. When you keep an Angel Journal, you are showing commitment to your Angels. You are showing commitment to your spiritual path. As you write you release your fears and anxieties and this helps you to calm your thoughts and your mind.

Your Angelic journal helps you to record events that have brought you happiness, contentment and joy, whilst working with your Angels to gain clarity and focus. Regular journaling shows the Angels your dedication.

The activity or regular writing demonstrates the qualities of releasing, expressing being joyful, being clear, having dedication, being grateful. These are all activities and qualities that help to raise your vibration, or the energy around you. These are all activities and qualities that help your aura and vibrational energy to become finer and purer.

As your mind becomes calmer, so your heart can become more full with love. In the presence of love a healing begins. In the calmness you are now able to really hear what your intuition has been trying to tell you. You hear the voice of your heart.

With a heart full of love the Angels can reach you. They can reach you because you are now emitting the energy of, peace, contentment and gratitude!

The Angel Journal is an essential tool in your development towards seeing, hearing, feeling and knowing your Angels. Remember to always write down and date your experiences. Over time you will look back and you will see how far you have come. Start your journey with the Angels today.

Call upon your Angels

When we have a lot of things going on in our lives we can sometimes forget to ask our Angels to come in to help us. Don't forget to ask your Angels, when you start to feel overwhelmed.

Remember to sit down regularly with the intention of just talking, thinking or writing with your Angels. Do these things from your heart! Say all the things that are currently causing you to feel overwhelmed it doesn't matter how big or small the solution seems to you, just tell everything to your friend, your Angel.

You can say anything. Your Angel does not judge you, but just listens and looks at you with a heart full of unconditional love. Remember any tears are medicine for the soul.

When you have said everything that is concerning you. Thank your Angel and take a breather. Go for a walk, or a swim. Take a warm bath or a refreshing shower, whatever you feel you need to do right now just do it. You may need to sleep for a little while to rest. Then come back to your meeting with your Angelic Journal and begin to write.

How to write your Angelic Journal

You are going to write everything down with your Angel present. You are going to write down all the things that really make your heart sing, all the little things for which you are grateful.

You have food, you have fresh water, you have electricity, you have the love of your family. Continue writing until you cannot think of anything more. Now, ask your Angel to go to someone who is in need. Someone who does not have all the things for which your currently feel grateful. Thank your Angels. Take another breather.

In the next session with your Angel, I would like you to try to develop some clarity. Become clear about how you really want your life to look, deep in your heart! What do you consider to be your ideal life, feel it!

Write about this ideal life now in your Angelic Journal. Believe that whatever is in your heart is coming into your life.

The Angels will hear you. The Angels will send you a sign. Be open to synchronicities. Know that whatever you have requested from you heart, *for the highest good of all concerned,* will manifest. It is Divine Law.

Start a regular programme of deep breathing and relaxation with your Angels this will help your requests to manifest more quickly.

Know that with the love of your Angels everything will be ok. Just take things at your own pace. There is no rush with healing. Just go with the flow, do each step when it feels right. When it feels right, this will be the Angels, teaching you how to listen to your intuition.

Successful week with Angelic Journaling

'After you suggested to keep an angel journal, and to write down the things I was praying for, I wrote down Wood (to heat my house), food, to feed my family & help with dentist for my son. That's all I wrote.

The next day a friend who cuts down trees stopped by with two loads of wood-he had no use for it and wondered if we wanted it!

The day after that two wonderful friends stopped by and not only brought us food, but made us dinner and organized my kitchen! My son has gotten medicine and going to the oral surgeon on Friday-(I found a sponsor)!!!

I am so thankful and grateful!!! I am blessed! What a wonderful feeling. I wish I could share it! Thank you for your inspiration. Thank you angels!! '

Hello what a fantastic week you have had with your Angels! I have a brimming smile! You are now well on your way. if you haven't already started this process, then start to meditate now to get to know your Guardian Angel more closely.   Then deeper work can begin. Thank you for sharing with us, very heart warming. Blessings to you and your family, as always. Michelle

Develop Clarity

What defines the flow of our life

Our life is directed by energy, thought energy. This includes thoughts about yourself, your current beliefs, understanding and programming. You are also affected by the thought energy and consciousness of others around you. The path of your life is smoother when you have thoughts of peace. The path is smoother when you set out in any direction with faith. The path of life is smoother when you walk with the love, protection and guidance of Angels.

You can create a smoother future for yourself and others through your thought energy in each and every moment. Create a path of peace, a path of love and a path of evolution for you and for everyone. The Angels will support you.

Where there is positive thought
There are Angels

Angels of Clarity

The Angels of Clarity can help you to change your life and achieve much more and grow. If you are not clear about what you want, then you send out mixed energies. The effect of mixed energies creates a feeling of being stuck. When you are stuck you end up going round and round in circles. The frustrations continue as you are walking through life with no direction.

The Angels of clarity can help you if you want to move forward and feel like you are stuck. The Angels of clarity can help you if you feel that your life is chaotic with no direction. They can help you if you have lost your enthusiasm and motivation.

When you create more clarity the Angels hear you and they make it their intention to help you manifest your desires.

To become clearer:

- Sit for a moment and still your mind
- Ask yourself *'What can I do, when I know that the Angels will help me to succeed'*? *'What would I do, if I knew that I couldn't fail'*?
- Write down a list of how your life would look

Once you are clear ask the Angels of Clarity:

For help with those things on your list
To help you release any fears, doubts or thoughts that no longer resonate with the energies of success

Only request things that are for *'the highest good of all concerned'*

Know that the Angels of Clarity have heard your requests and are now already finding ways to arrange for these things to manifest. Remember to thank the Angels.

It is very important that you go about your life in the comfort and knowledge that these requests have now gone on the wings of your Angels. The Angels are now busy manifesting your Hearts Desire's. Know that all requests are heard, even if they are delivered to you, in a different form to what you imagined.

Angels hear your emotion

Angels hear your emotion and respond. When you write to your Angels, it is not the words that you write that are important, but the emotions that they evoke in your heart.

Emotions create a resonance, a vibration. Angels hear, feel and see vibrations. Where your requests are made from your heart, and not from your head, then they are expressed with heartfelt love. Angels always respond to the vibration and emotion of love.

Still you mind and become calm and clear. Now write to your Angels from your heart. The Angels will hear you and they will respond. Look for the presence of your Angels as they will provide a sign or a synchronicity.

Sit down in a quiet place where there are no distractions. This is your time.

- Listen to some inspiring or calming music to help you open your heart and write more easily
- Light a candle and some incense to create a peaceful ambience around you
- Start to breathe deeply and feel relaxed
- Start to write to your Angels, tell them everything that is on your mind. You can tell your Angel anything, your Angel holds no judgment. Your Angel is your friend Supreme. State the things that are causing you fear, agitation, worry, pain. Keep writing, let everything just flow out, remember that tears are healing for your soul
- Feel the anxieties lifting from you as you continue to write
- Everything you have written can now be handed over to your Angels. Imagine them taking your concerns on their wings to the heart of God. They are now taking everything to be healed.
- Thank your Angels for being with you today. Say *'Thank your dear Angels for hearing me today'*.
- Now take some time. You may decide to go for a walk, to take a warm bath, to drink some fresh water. Do whatever feels refreshing and comforting for you.

When you have taken some time to rest, you will feel more refreshed and relaxed. Return to your journal.   You are now going to write to your Angels about your Heart's Desires.
Write down and date your experiences.

I begged my Angel...... but nothing!

Tried my hardest, even begged for my angel to help me be calm, and feel peace through a very tough moment...nothing....I don´t know if just certain people can feel them or see them from what I have read....???? I will keep trying though. I will always believe!!

To call an Angel you call from a Heart of Love. You say *'Angel, please be with me now, and enfold me in your loving wings'*.

If you cry out, whilst begging, because you are frustrated, then you are not coming from you heart, but from the demands of your personality - Angels find it difficult to come close, if your aura is discordant.

The next time you need Angelic Assistance, make time to stop! Speak with emotion from your heart, not from you little self. Your little self is your personality. We cannot command Angels, we can only Ask Angels from our heart of love, peace, trust and belief. Your Angel will then come closer to you.

Look for the things around that you have to be grateful for ....
Look at the things in your life that are frustrating you and say *'thank you'*.

Without these experiences you may not think of your Angels or look deeper at your life. These experiences are teaching you.

Sometimes when we are becoming more spiritually mature our Angel steps back. Your Angel has not gone away and is still protecting you. But your Angel is now confident that for this part of your journey, you can do it alone.

If you stumble and fall your Angel is there, loving you unconditionally. But for this moment you may walk tall, and strong. Say *'I am a child of God, and today I choose to walk in my strength, my own personal power. Today I choose to walk with love in your heart, each and every step. My Angel is with me'.* Blessings Michelle

Where there is a will, there is a way

Angels can only come as close as we allow them to be. Where there is a will there is a way. When you have the willingness to meet your Angels and call them into your life, then they will automatically surrender to your requests. The Angels will set about to find solutions immediately. Angels love to serve.

Hearts Desires

Our Hearts Desires are exactly that! They are the Desires of our Heart! As such, we do not strive to seek them, instead we need to *feel* them. As we *feel* the things in our Heart that bring us peace and contentment, then we are no longer striving. Instead we are Being!

It is in the Being that we Become

What does your heart really desire?

Feel in your heart for a few moments the things that you truly desire, the things that truly make you feel peaceful, calm and relaxed. Now begin to write again in your Angelic Journal.

Imagine your ideal situation, your ideal life
Imagine it right now, as if you already have it, really feel it in your heart
Write down how this ideal life looks as if you have it NOW!

Write down your desires one by one

I am now living in my ideal home
I am now abundant in all things
I am healthy and vibrant now
I am happy and healthy
I am vibrant and filled with happy and healthy energy
I am totally healed on all levels now
I am now living in my peace

I am now working on a project, job assignment which fills me with passion
I am now able to share my skills, time, love and passion with others
I now have a loving relationship with myself and others
My partner and I are in love and cherish and honour each moment together

Keep writing your ideal situation, write it in as much detail as you can, feel every detail, see it, sense it, smell it. How do you feel in this ideal situation? Keep writing. Now say *'Angels, may this or something greater now manifest for the highest good of all concerned'*

Hand everything over to the Angels, know that your requests have been heard and that solutions are already on their way to you. Thank your Angels and go about your day. Keep looking for the signs and synchronicities that will be now presented to you, to show you that your Angels are with you.

An Angels Love is an Eternal Tone

An Angel has an eternal tone
Vibrating in the wind, like a bell leading you home
When you follow the sounds of the ethereal chiming...
All your Hearts Desires will be created in perfect and Divine Timing

I would love something good to come my way

'I Would love some think good to come my way fed of having bad luck all the time have asked loads iv time for help may be one day my life will change for the better'

Hello, sit down with your Angelic Journal and write to your Angels. Write from you heart. Tell them everything, let it all out. Then go for a little walk or break.

Now come back to your Angel Journal and ask the Angels for help with everything that you need. Ask for your hearts desire's, let the Angels hear your passion, and emotions.

Now say *'May this or something greater manifest for the highest good of all concerned'.*
Thank your Angels. Go about your day. Look for your signs and synchronicities.

Over time you will look at your journal and you will see how far you have come and how much help you have actually received. Thank your Angels. Let me know how you get along. Blessings Michelle

---

There are many roads

There are many roads
There are many choices
How can you decide?

You call upon your Angels
You state your concerns

You listen to the feelings in your heart as you go through your options. The options that fill you heart with passion, enthusiasm, love and positive energies are the right options. These are the options of your hearts desires.

Never doubt your heart
Angels speak to us through our intuition which we hear in the feelings of our Heart

Write a Prayer

How to write a Prayer to your Angel

Prayers devised from a person's **soul,** from a person's own intention to reach out, these are the **most powerful** forms of Prayer available.
A **Prayer** written by another person is fine, so long as when you read it, or say it, you **feel it** in your **heart**; you feel it in your **emotions.**

Angels are the messengers of you're your God. The Angels hear and feel the emotions of your prayers. They feel it like a vibration or a resonance, an energy. It prompts them to respond to you.

Angels respond with, **Signs, Synchronicities and MIRACLES!**

Sit peacefully, calm and still
Feel the emotions in your heart
Now call upon the Angels, *'Dear Angels, from my position of heart felt love please can you help me now with ……'*

Thank your Angel in the knowledge that today; a healing has taken place, in your heart.

Pray to your Angels

Praying to your angel can help you to heal

To say a prayer you first connect with your heart. Once connected with your heart, you can set your intention. If your intention is pure and comes from a position of integrity, then the heart opens.

As the heart opens, its magnificent light, beams outwards. It expands far and wide and is heard by the Universe. The Universe hears this as a sound, a vibration, an energy.

This energy having been directed from your heart is Unconditional Love. The Angels hear, feel and know this sound and in that moment are automatically drawn to you. The Angels are themselves, the energy of Unconditional Love. Like attracts like.

As Angels approach you, they see that your heart is open. Your heart is open because of your prayers. They beam their energy of unconditional love directly into your heart centre.
In that moment a healing occurs. Healing is the result of
receiving unconditional love. You may feel it. Your replenished heart will now resonate a feeling of peace, clarity and love.

Thank your Angels, for their heartfelt gift. Today you can walk confidently in the knowledge that another aspect of your life has been healed.

Where there is Unconditional Love
There is a Healing
Where there is a Healing
There are Angels!

How often should we speak to our Angels?

Speak with your Angels every moment, every thought, every word, every breath, every day!
The more you think breath or talk about Angels, the easier it is for them to reach you.

Your thoughts of Angels
The sound of the word Angel
The relaxation you feel when you breathe, acknowledging your Angel

These actions all provide a pure vibrating resonance around you, which the Angels can hear feel and see.

When you are radiating a peaceful aura, then the Angels can reach you more easily. They will be able to extend their light outwards. These extensions of light form Angelic wings, which then enfold you and nurture you. A profound moment. A moment of peace.

Where there is Peace
There are Angels!

Affirmations

An Affirmation is a mantra, which is repeated over and over. The repetition of an affirmation can help the mind to believe, that what it is hearing, is its current reality.
The mind realigns itself in accordance to the new energy being produced by the positive affirmation or mantra.

The realignment of your energy has a positive and direct impact upon your aura. The aura is the invisible protective energy shield that we all embody. The aura becomes smoother, finer and purer. Angels can approach you easier when you have a fine smooth aura.

The Universe hears your aura as a vibration a sound, an energy. The Universe automatically realigns itself to match the new thoughts that are producing this resonance. Like attracts Like.

Affirmations are best said in the present, the *now*. Affirmations are best said as if you have already received or achieved them e.g. I am *now* healthy, healing energy flows to me *now*, easily and effortlessly.

Have clarity about those areas of your life that you want to change. Then combine this clarity with affirmations and write them in your prayers to your Angels. With the help of the Angels wondrous Miracles, can and do happen.

Examples of Affirmations that you can combine with your Prayers

I am now able to see, hear, feel and know the presence of my Guardian Angel
I now experience the wonder and love of Angels in all my relationships
I thank you Angels for now being a valuable part of my life in every moment
I am now fully healed on all levels
I now have an abundance of vibrant energy
I am now healed physically, emotionally, spiritually and psychologically
I now only speak with honesty, truth and integrity in all my dealings
I am now working in a job which fills me with passion
I now have a continuous stream of financial resources
I am now able to help my child through my extra energy and dedication to parenting
I have now written a book about Angels which reaches many people. The book helps them to experience the love, protection and nurturing of Angels in their own lives

In your Angelic Journal write headings for all aspects of your life. Write how you would like each of them to improve. Try to devise as many affirmations as possible so that they can be used in conjunction with your daily prayers.

Possible headings:

Work
Health
Love
Spiritual
Home
Friends
Environment
Children
Animals
Clarity
Education
Abundance: Wisdom, Inspiration, Creativity, Compassion, Patience
How can I serve?

Now write a list of how you can practically help yourself to achieve some of these goals and aspirations. Improving these aspects of your life will also help to increase your self-love and self-esteem.

Once you have written your affirmations and prayers go about your day. Be happy in the knowledge that your Angels have heard you. Know that the energies around you are realigning and that a positive flow will follow from your God and the Angels. Remember to thank your Angels for your Blessings as and when they arrive.

Summary of steps

- Clarity
- Open heart and integrity

- Call in the Angels
- Affirmations combined with prayers
- Personal action towards you goals

Things will now happen in the exact right moment with Divine Timing.

Divine Timing

Whenever we speak to our Angels and ask for their help we are always heard. The Angels always help us. If there is a seeming delay between when you make your requests and their manifestation, this may be because:

It allows you more time to become clear about what you really need
It allows you time to work on the qualities within your own heart, so that you are ready to receive these Divine Gifts and blessings when they arrive

There may be something better in store for you, which can only be seen from a higher perspective

There are 3 answers to requests, yes, not now, and no. No may mean is something better in store for you

Look for your opportunities as they are presented to you. They may be ideas urging you to write, or to meet someone, or to join a local club for example. Listen to your intuition and accept all opportunities as they are presented to you.

Things happen in the exact right moment with Divine timing, go with the flow

---

Divine Timing

A concerto is composed one note at a time
A tree grows one branch at a time
A flower opens one petal at a time
Our journey to Heaven unfolds one step at a time

Don't try to push or struggle with the flow, the beat, the natural rhythm
Everything is synchronised by Divine timing
So be in the beat

Be in the moment
Step by step

Manifestation

How things manifest

Should I plan my life or just go with the flow? The answer is, you can work with both.

Make your Plan

The plan helps you to set your **intentions**
The plan helps you to **focus on the things that need to be done to get to your goals**
The plan helps you to list the **skills,** the **aspirations** and **knowledge** you may need to get to your desired outcome

The **Angels** will see your plans from a **higher perspective. The Angels hear you call upon them with your plan,** your **hearts desires and your dreams**. They will immediately set about finding the solutions and answers.

Going with the flow

Release any attachment that you hold towards how these goals will **manifest**. Instead, **focus** in that **moment**, on the very **next thing** you need to do in order to achieve your **overall plan.**

Ask the Angels
Believe in the Angels

Trust the **Angels** to deliver any solutions in a perfect way for you and *'for the greatest good of all concerned'*.

The process of Manifestation

The unmanifest world is the place where all our thoughts and energies reside. With Divine timing these energies become reality.

To manifest the life that your heart desire's, then feel today in your heart what it would feel like to have all the things, the life, the emotions that you truly desire. Imagine the feeling of seeing, hearing and knowing your Angel.

Write down all these thoughts, feelings and emotions. The Angels are there to help you. Ask them to take these thoughts and energies on their wings to the heart of your God. Go about your day, your week your life. The Universe holds the blueprint for the higher perspective.

With Divine Timing your heart's desires will manifest! Stay open to them appearing in a different form to how you may have imagined them, as the heart of your God holds the highest potential and outcomes for all. All prayers, emotions, thoughts are answered.

Be open to receiving
Be open to hearing
Be open to seeing

Remember to thank your Angels daily for the work and Miracles that they may undertake in the unmanifest realms. Feel blessed when you receive your heart's desires.

Miracles!

The Angels see everything from a higher perspective and they know if there is a greater plan for you. As your synchronicities unfold, write them down. Know that all prayers requested from the heart are answered.

Be sure to act upon any opportunities that may present themselves. When you have demonstrated complete faith and integrity know that miracles, can and do happen.

Look for your **signs, synchronicities and opportunities**. **Doors will open.** Your plan is **manifesting.** When your answers arrive, t**hank your Angels**

Where there are heart felt prayers.
There are Angels
Where there are Angels
Miracles can and do happen!

Why is my partner not coming?

When I ask for that someone to come back into my life how come has not happen for me dose god of the lovely angel not care I am just a bad woman I would not do anything to any body or dogs/cats so why I am life behind all the time I am saying this from the heart love x

In your Angel Journal write down all the things you would like in your partner, only write positive things. Now feel in your heart what these qualities would look like for you in your life. Say *'may this or something greater now manifest, for the highest good of all concerned'*. Thank the Angels.

Now, the important thing is to let it go. Let the Angels take your requests to the heart of your God. In the meantime, look at the list of qualities you have written and keep working on those qualities for yourself.

Keep giving love from your heart. Look for the signs and synchronicities around you that show to you that love is being returned. Don't forget to also love yourself in direct proportion to how you would like someone else to love you.

When you feel loved and peaceful from whatever source, then the Universe hears these feelings and send you more of the same. Love yourself as if you were being loved by your Soul mate. Blessings as always. Michelle

I asked for a relationship, why hasn't it manifested?

Angels can reach you more easily and more quickly, when you have complete trust, faith and belief in their abilities. Trust Faith Belief!

Angels can and do love support and protect you in all ways. If you have made a request and it has not yet manifested then this is maybe because the pieces are being put into place. The Angels may also have something better for you, they see the overall plan.

For example, if you have asked for a partner, then you will have already written everything down, and you will have felt in your total being how it would be to have this partner. You will have given some time for this to manifest. During the time you are waiting, you can continue to work further on developing in yourself, some of the qualities you seek in another.

Your soul mate may not yet be in a position to be with you. He or she may be in a different place emotionally, spiritually, physically. With Divine timing and the work of the Angels, this partner or relationship will manifest.

Each day you can say *'I am now happily with my soul mate'*

Then go about your normal routine, in the full inner knowledge that your requests have been heard by the Angels. Walk to work confidently as if you already have your partner. Feel it in your heart. Smile. Relax, trust and believe. This will help you to hold the vibration of feeling love longer and longer. The Angels hear your vibrations and send you more of the same. With Divine timing your relationship will manifest, if it is for the highest good of all concerned.

Thank the Angels. You know the blessing of love is already on its way to you. It is on its way even though it may appear to you in a different form to how you imagined. Love attracts Love. Like attracts Like.

What if my Hearts Desires are not for my highest good?

What if my ideal life and what I may desire is not for my highest good? I think it is and I really want it and believe strong it will come to pass. But what if my ideal life is actually not for my highest good? Will it be denied me?

You can have whatever your Heart desire's as long as it doesn't negate anything that the soul has previously agreed to undertake during this incarnation. Keep clear in your heart those qualities of love, joy and peace. These emotions can only ever create things for the highest good of all concerned.

My Life is dire.....

Michelle please can you advise, I have some crystals, but my life is dire, no job, bad health & mentally all over the place, I am trying to focus my energy's but I'm wondering if I'm doing something wrong? At the mo I use daily Healing with the Angels cards every day, any help is much appreciated x

To find your way dear one, you first need to just **STOP! Stop and listen!** What do you feel in your heart? **Write** this now **to your Angel**, every **detail,** all your pain and worries. Let everything flood out. **Tears are medicine** for the soul. Then take a **breather. G**o out for a walk and just **breathe everything out.**

Now, sit down in a quiet, **serene place. Write** down your **perfect life**, every **detail**. How does it feel, how does it smell, how does it look. **Talk** about it as if you already live this life! **Imagine it! Feel it!**

Write these feelings of joy, peace, laughter into the new picture of your life The new life that you now deserve. With the **Angels** you know that with **belief** you can't fail.

Now say *'May this or something greater manifest for the greatest good of all concerned'.*
On your fridge stick a note *'Today, is the first day of the rest of my life'.*
Thank your Angels, go about your life **glowing!** Glowing because **you believe** in the **Angels**.

Say *'Today, I recognise and feel the love of my Angel'. **Stop!*** What do you feel now?
Your Angels wings are firmly wrapped around you. Write everything in your **Angelic Journal**
This is your moment!

*Where there are **Angels***
***Miracles** can and do happen!*

Where in the Bible does it say to pray to Angels?

Can't we just go right to Jesus himself for healing???? Where in the Bible does it say we are to pray to angels? Yes, they are real. Yes, they protect us. Yes they are sent by God. But they are NOT Deity and this page acts like they are. To me that's blasphemy. And if we are to pray, it is not in the name of 'light and love' but by Jesus' name only are we to pray.

Hello how lovely to meet you here today. You are indeed correct that Angels are not deity and as such should not be worshipped. However, Angels are messengers of your God and are made in the essence of your God. When you call upon God, if that is your belief, then he would send his Angels as his messengers to help you and assist you.

Healing happens when you receive the energy of unconditional love and as such we ask the Angels for healing as they are themselves beacons of unconditional love. I think the main focus is not who we are praying to but more the intention we hold in our heart when we pray. Then the appropriate energy which resonates most perfectly for you, will be brought forward, whether that be God, Jesus, Angels, Buddha, Mohammed etc etc. Angels help everyone, regardless of their religion, beliefs or culture. The reason people talk with such admiration about Angels is because they have in many cases had their lives profoundly changed by meeting them or sensing them. Please keep in touch. Your viewpoint is greatly appreciated. Blessings dear one. Michelle

I saw an image of myself with Angel Wings

Hi Michelle - hope that you're still well :) I don't know what is happening to me though (if what I'm feeling is part of The Shift or not) but today I went to the St George's Cathedral in Cape Town for an Anglican sermon (My first one ever though - I'm used to the Dutch Reformed Church). The reason why I went to this cathedral is that I wasn't in my usual church for quite some time now... While the sermon was on, I got the sensations what I always feel when I'm in meditation - the tingling sensation I got (and even more sensations, ears ringing as well) with a difference; it is as if it went through the charts - it's nonstop. I don't know if it is the Angels are trying to say something to me... I'll also admit (which I didn't share before because I was afraid and thought it cannot be) is that when I first started with the guardian angel meditation, I thought I saw myself with longish dark hair (which I actually had for a few years for real) and wings. I shook that image off and tried the meditation again and yet again it was me... but this version of me was much more confident, I could see it in his (or my?) eyes and smile (? or was it a smirk?). I'm just confused... Well here is the link - Have a great week, Blessings to you.

Hello Roean, well as you know the tingling is definitely your Angels touch and the ringing in your ears is the Angels opening your ear chakras so that you can hear them more clearly and open your clairaudience. The vision of you with wings was indeed true also. When the time is right we are given our Angel wings and you were being shown how you yourself exhibit the qualities of an Angel on Earth. I am fascinated by your family heritage and will take some time later to look at your link. Don't worry about which church you do or don't visit. Remember your church is in your heart. Thank you so much for sharing your wonderful experience, remember to write all your progress in your Angelic Journal. Over time you will see how far you have indeed progressed. Once you engage in a path with the Angels then you go through periods of enhanced transitions and progress and this is what you are currently experiencing. Just go with the flow and enjoy learning with your Angelic team. Have trust in what you see, hear and feel. When you work with the Angels you are safe and protected as they just want you to hear, see and feel their love. Embrace it! Now is your time to ask the Angels for your answers. They will start to show you the things that you need to know..... Blessings dear one as always... Michelle

Connecting with your Guardian Angel

Your Guardian Angel is waiting for you to make a connection. Your Guardian Angel is always reaching out his or her hand to you. As soon as you think about making a connection with your Guardian Angel he or she is already sending beams of unconditional love towards you. These beams of unconditional love help you hear, feel, sense or see.

By regularly taking some time to work with your Guardian Angel, in meditation or contemplation, you will receive an Angelic attunement. This opens you up to the healing power of your Angels. You will no longer fear the illusions of pain, suffering or separation. You will begin to understand that in fact, everything is love. With your permission your Guardian Angel will teach you every step of the way.

How to meditate to meet your Guardian Angel

Meditation undertaken in a dedicated space or room, at a regular time will help your mind and senses to quickly acquire the skills of peace, serenity and tranquillity.

Meditation Essentials

- Your meditation room should be comfortably warm and clean of clutter
- Open a window slightly
- Choose a regular time to practise meditation – dawn or dusk are most effective
- Make sure you will not be disturbed for at least 30 minutes
- Make a simple altar as a focus point
- Make yourself comfortable with pillows, rugs and cushions
- Have an extra layer of clothing or a blanket to cover yourself as your temperature may drop during meditation

Meditation Preparation

- Light a candle and /or incense
- Play some soothing Angelic or relaxing music
- Use essential oils in a burner, or a room spray
- Place fresh flowers in your meditation room

- Take a shower or bath and put on clean clothes before you begin
- Wear loose comfortable clothing preferably pastel colours or white
- Hold a crystal

Meditation Posture

- Sit cross-legged or in the lotus yoga position on the floor
- Put a cushion under you so that your pelvis is tilted slightly forward
- Keep your back straight but relaxed
- If your prefer to sit in a chair then choose a straight backed chair and make sure your feet are flat on the floor
- Rest your palms upwards in your lap or rest your palms down on your knees
- If you prefer you can lie flat in the sleep posture

Grounding

- Once you are comfortable imagine that you have roots growing out of the soles of your feet
- Imagine these roots growing deeply and firmly into the earth below you until they reach the centre of the earth
- If you are seated, you can also imagine additional roots growing from the base of your spine into the earth
- Feel the vast Universe above your head

Relax

- Now take some time to focus on your breathing…..
- Breathe in to the word love
- Breathe out to the word peace
- In love, out peace
- Continue in a pattern that is comfortable for you until you start to feel relaxed
- Just allow any passing thoughts to come and go…..
- Relax all your muscles one by one

Begin your journey

Imagine your ideal scene. For example:
- Walking in a meadow
- Sitting on a hill
- Lying by the river
- Standing overlooking the sea

Call in your Angel

Now say in your mind or out loud, *'Guardian Angel, please come closer to me. Please help me to recognise the signs of your presence'*

Allow your journey to unfold

Continue to relax in your ideal scene in your inner world. Continue to breathe steadily in and out…

- Become aware of all sensations

- Be aware of any impressions or ideas in your mind
- Notice any smells, colours or pictures in your mind
- Notice your feelings of joy and peace

Finish the meditation

As the feelings and impressions subside:
- Write everything down in your Angelic Journal
- Thank your Guardian Angel
- Go about your day
- Be open to and aware of receiving personal signs and synchronicities from your Angel

Each time you repeat this visualisation your relationship with your Angel will become stronger. *Your Guardian Angel is your Friend Supreme.*

Questions about connecting with your Guardian Angel

Could definitely use a guiding hand at times with connecting?

Hello, the best thing that I have found for connecting is a guided visualisation and meditation to meet your Guardian Angel. Use any meditation that feels right for you. When you use a visualisation regularly, your body and its senses learn how to become relaxed. As they become trained for relaxation, then it becomes easier and easier to feel your Angel's presence.

The process, of going to a special place in your home or office, just for the purpose of talking with your Angels, is important. Lighting a candle, putting on some soothing music and writing in your Angelic Journal; these are all activities that train the body and senses that it is now time to be calm and peaceful.

The Angels love calm and peace and can now move closer to you. In time you will have trained your senses sufficiently to be able to just sit anywhere and make the connection. Just go one step at a time. The Angels always hear you, so nothing is ever lost when taking time to work with them. Let me know how you get along. Blessings dear one. Michelle

To tune into your Angels you need to find their wave length

I have spent a lot of time meditating. Here are some of the results I have had. I asked my spirit guide to make themselves known to me. Our of the 'blur' stepped a most beautiful Native American woman. I did not hear a

voice so I do not know if this is the one who I have heard say my name
....

I asked my Guardian Angel to make themselves known to me. Out of the blur stepped a very tall image, light brownish little longer than shoulder length hair. Although, I saw a face and can still picture the face they never came all the way out of the blur and then went back into it. I got the feeling that I was just not meant to fully see my Angel yet.

The frequency of spirit guides and Angels is very different. If you call your Angels you will be requesting to be taken to another frequency and vibration. You must also match this vibration within yourself.

Imagine the Spirit Guides are on one radio station, which is local radio and then imagine the Angels are on another waveband far away. To tune into them you need to follow the routes of peace, love and joy.

In meditation call in your Guardian Angel only! Now take notice of what you feel, sense smell, if you get a strong connection then ask the Angel for a name, ask the Angel to say your name, so that you can get used to how they feel!

Remember, that everything we see in meditation is only as helpful as our understanding of it. So write everything in your Angelic Journal and take small regular steps to build up this relationship with your Guardian Angel. Purify your home, your heart and your vibration simultaneously. The Angels are with you and with a little more purification they will be able to reach you. I am looking forward to hearing how you get along.

I saw a white flash, was it my Guardian Angel?

I recently had a flash of DeyJa Vu.. It was a figure of white.. not menacing but friendly and wise.. was this my Guardian Angel

Hello, how lovely to meet you here today. The white flash may well of been a sign from an Angel. To know your Guardian Angel you need to first get used to working with him or her. Firstly call out and ask for a sign of their presence. Then work with all your senses through meditation, visualisation and contemplation until you have recognised the exact way your Guardian Angel reaches out to you. Please follow the meditation called 'Meet your Guardian Angel' regularly, and write down in your Angelic Journal everything that you experience at the end of the session. Little by little you will learn to know your Guardian Angel and the connection will become stronger and stronger. Blessings to you... Enjoy your Journey. Michelle

How meeting your Guardian Angel can feel

Dear Michelle! Thank You for Your interested! :)My meditation was very heart -stiring,my tears run, and I feel very airy! Be honest, my power of imagination is very weak,so,that all this beautiful places, flowers,(even gold :)) I have not seen...I could not even find out the name of my Guardian Angel...But this feeling....O:)!!!! I am blessed...Thank You once more!

This is wonderful news! This means that the Angel is opening your heart, and in that moment tears of joy and love just flow. The feeling of being light is your Guardian Angel wrapping you in the healing essence of unconditional love. Be in no doubt that this is your Guardian Angel. Thank you so much for letting me know. What a lovely start to the week for me. Me and my Angels are beaming with smiles. Blessings dear one. Walk in peace.

My Guardian Angel came to me

After I saw THIS, I Had to tell you about my experience!!! Yesterday I was doing a 'guided' meditation I found & quite by accident, It was one to help me get closer to my guardian angel & find out her name..during that time,

She came to me just as I remember her many many years ago when I was in a car accident at 16! So Beautiful With LONG Beautiful Loose Golden Curls. I can still Feel Her Warmth when I'm Typing this or think of her..so moving on, She just said "Lauren." (sounds kind of young & hip for a guardian angel right!? lol) & handed me a stone and turned and walked away into a fog like until she disappeared..

when I opened my hand it was a beautiful rose quartz..One I had recognized as one of my own! I retrieved it from where I keep it as I feel She Was Telling Me I Needed This Particular Stone..One of Unconditional Love & Self Love.. I had been beating myself up over something I had no control over..Could That Have Been Her Message? BTW I haven't let my stone go since.

What a beautiful meeting with your Guardian Angel. I think it is a strong sign from your Guardian Angel that the Rose Quartz crystal is an important step in protecting and healing your heart. Thank you so much for sharing this with us. Blessings as always, Michelle

---

I keep thanking my Guardian Angel

This summer I almost lost my husband to an anaphylactic shock episode after we were attacked by an angry nest of yellow jackets during a hike with my family.

The night before I had a dream my son drowned. But I ignored it and still decided the next morning to go on our planned nature hike but stay away from any nature hikes involving water. We ended up on a landing near a waterfall when it all took place.

All I remember is that a car with 2 people just so happened to stop where we were and helped us get help. We were in a very deserted place.

I still believe the man who stopped was an angel. All I keep thinking about and thanking is my guardian angel and how lucky I am to have her.

Through the whole ordeal I felt guidance and a sense of calm, and I couldn't see everyone around (all the assistance) all I felt was the presence of many angels surrounding and protecting all of us. I believe.

Is it my Guardian Angel calling my name?

I often hear someone calling my name when I am by myself. Is it my Guardian Angel?

Go into a calm relaxed state and ask your Guardian Angel for his/her name, take the first name you are given. Now ask the Angel to call your name, notice his/her presence, if the presence feels loving and comforting and if you hear your name called the same way as when you were alone, then you will know it is your Guardian Angel.

Why do some people see Angels?

I talk with the Angels All the time, Maybe one day i will be able to see them, i wonder though why some people can see them than others, have you physically seen Angels Michele?

Hello, I see, hear, feel and know Angels but I have also trained all my senses to be able to do this on an on-going basis. I now channel the wisdom of the Angels in most of my postings and responses.

It is possible for everyone to see Angels, but it is a process. In most cases, it is a process of spiritual awakening on many levels.

You can ask the Angels to allow you to see them. Try teaching your third eye to see Angels during your meditations. You can do this by asking the Angels that you may now be able to use your clairvoyance.

Remember, visions by people who say they are clairvoyant does not necessarily equal wisdom but with the aid of your Angels then everything you may see and experience will be both wise, loving and nurturing. Blessings to you as always, Michelle

Section 6

Angel Signs

Angel Signs

You do not have to be a clairvoyant or psychic to sense the presence of your Angels. Angels are just waiting for you to call them. They are always reaching out to you, this is their purpose.

When you believe in Angels, you are demonstrating that you believe in love, peace, safety and healing. By believing in these qualities your Angel can draw closer to you and reach out a hand to guide and receive you.
You only have to believe and you only have to ask! The Angels will always hear and respond to any request with a sign, a synchronicity or a miracle! Be open to hear see, feel and know your Angels every day.

Request that an Angel come close. Angels cannot intervene without your permission.
The more you call upon the Angels the more you will sense a connection to them. Your connection will become stronger and stronger.
Your Angels rejoice when you ask them for their assistance. No task is too big or too small. Your **Angels** can help you **shop for presents**, or to **travel safely** to your destination. Your Angels can **introduce** you to
the **people** and ideas that you need in your life. People and ideas that you may need in order to progress at this time. **Angels** create synchronicities, opportunities and Miracles!

To sense the Angels, you need to understand that you are worthy of hearing, feeling or seeing an Angel. Everyone has an Angel and everyone is worthy of having a relationship with their Angel.

To make it easier for an Angel to reach you then try to ask the Angels for help with anything and everything regularly, daily! Sit in a calm still environment like your Angel Sanctuary and still your mind. Call upon your Angels. Say *'I would like to feel my Guardian Angel now'!*

The Angels will always hear and respond to any request

Angel Experiences – who has those?

Everyone has had an Angel experience. It is impossible, to not have had one! It is impossible because we all have a Guardian Angel with us throughout every incarnation.

Maybe the thing that is amiss, is your awareness of your Angels, when they are around you? All those times your heart has cried out, your Angels were with you. Every time you were joyful your Angel was there with you. Every time you are awake and every night when you are asleep your Angel is there with you.

Train your awareness to see, feel, hear and know the signs and presence of your Angels. Learn to be in your peace. Learn to create the correct atmosphere for Angels to reach you.

Remember, to ask the Angels to come into your life. It is against Divine Law for Angels to intervene without your permission. They have no free-will.

You can call upon your Angels for help with everything and anything. Everyone is worthy. Angels love to serve, that is their purpose. As soon as you ask for assistance, your requests are immediately taken on the wings of Angels to your God. You will receive a sign or synchronicity either in that moment or at some future time.

Write everything in your Angelic Journal. Over time you will look back and you will see with open eyes that the Angels did hear you. You will open you heart wider as you now know that the love of Angels is indeed true. As you heart opens wider, the Angels draw ever close. The Angels walk with us all.

An Angel passed by your window

As an Angel passes by your window, you hear the gentle flutter
Its iridescent body of light, within the wings and the feathers

*As you gaze out to comprehend
You are left in awe
For in your sight, you can no longer pretend*

*Your Angel is standing there in its full Glory
The silence is profound
The moment is profound
The peace is profound*

*At this moment no level of your life returns to the mundane
You know without doubt
The feeling of Unconditional Love
The feeling of Safety
The Knowing that all is 'interconnected' and that you are never alone*

How to sense the presence of your Angels

When Angels draw closer you will find one or more of your five senses becoming more elevated. You may see, feel, taste, smell or hear subtle but profound sensations in and around your body.

Atmosphere

The atmosphere in the room may change and you may feel a tingling or goose bumps. The hairs on your arms may begin sticking up. You may feel a rush of energy in your body. You may feel warmth or energy in your heart or spine. You may sense a change in air pressure.

Smell

You may smell a sweet aroma like sublime perfume or flowers

Taste

You may have a distinct taste like sweetness

Feelings

You may have feelings of love and an overwhelming sense of peace and calm. Tears may flow because of extreme joy and emotional healing

Seeing

You may sense a coloured or a bright dazzling light, even if your eyes are closed

Hearing

You may hear the voice of your Angel. Believe the voice that you hear, it will sound like your own voice but it will be directed from your heart and not your head. It will always be loving.

Sensing

You may feel something brushing against you or enfolding you like a hug. These are Angel wings. You may sense a warm breeze or it may feel like someone is lightly touching your hair. You may become aware that something loving is sitting or standing close to you.

Synchronicities

You may start to see an increase in synchronicities in your life. There are no co-incidences. So any synchronicity in your life is the work of your Angel.

Solutions

You may find solutions to your problems in the most unexpected ways

Miracles

When you believe in Angels, miracles can and do happen! Never doubt, question or underestimate your ability or worthiness to receive. Where there are Angels, where there is complete trust belief and surrender, then miracles can and do happen! You only have to ask! Your Angels can only assist at your request.

Intuition

Angels talk to your heart through your intuition. If you are following a path based on love and not fear, then you are usually on the right track. The Angels will give you a sign to show you. There are no mistakes only learning's. If you make a decision and then find that you need to go another way, the Angels are with you to support and love you unconditionally. Angels allow you free will and will never tell you what to do. Instead, they will gently show you when you are on the right track. Listen to your heart. Ask the Angels to show you.

An Angel teaches your heart with Love
Where there are emotions
There are Angels
Listen to your heart and your emotions
Angels speak to you through your heart in the form of emotional intuition

To draw your Angels close to you

1. Go to your quiet place, light a candle and say *'today I would like to meet my Guardian Angel'*
2. Sit comfortably and slow your breathing
3. On the in breath say love. On the out breath say peace. Continue to slow your breathing. In love, out peace.
4. When you feel relaxed say in your mind *'Guardian Angel please show me a sign now'*
5. Keep breathing slowly and steadily. Notice anything in and around you, sensations, feelings, sounds, smells, changes in temperature, a slight breeze
6. Stay in this relaxed place until all sensations subside. Write down everything in your Angelic Journal
7. Thank your Guardian Angel
8. Blow out your candle and dedicate it to your Angel. Say *'I dedicate this candle to my Guardian Angel and our journey together'*
9. Go about your day

10. Look for signs from your Angels, synchronicities, feathers, words, songs.

An Angel's Love is like a gentle wave

An Angel's love is like a 'gentle wave upon the shore'
It makes the shingle glisten and twirl
It moves the most stubborn of rocks, moulding and caressing them until they are smooth
It purifies and washes away the old

An Angel's love is like a 'wave lapping on the shore'
Its sound is that of peace
Its presence that of calm
In its subtlety your Heart remember the 'love of greater things'

To know a 'wave lapping on the shore' is to know an Angel

Common Angelic Signs

Angels are just waiting to show us of their existence. When we call upon them they have many ways to show us a personal sign. They want us to know that they have heard us and are indeed with us.

These are just a few of the common signs, but the list is not exhaustive:
- Feathers appearing in a way that has meaning for you
- Clouds
- a song on the radio about Angels
- a word on a signpost as you drive
- a book falling off a shelf as you walk into a room
- finding coins
- someone talking to you about Angels
- someone telling you something that answers a question or problem that has been on your mind
- a stranger giving you appropriate advice
- the spontaneous love of an animal
- someone buying you an Angel related gift out of the blue
- seeing an image of an Angel or a feather e.g. on the TV, on a moving vehicle, on your computer screen

The list is endless and will always be personalised to mean something unique and special to the person receiving the sign. If you have been asking Angels to come into your life then be open to anything that is significant or personal to you. There are many ways the Angels use to let you know that they have heard you, and that they are with you.

Angels always hear you, and they always send you a sign

Angels bring messages to us during our sleep

Angels are usually invisible to us. They exist and vibrate at a finer and higher level of frequency than we can normally see. Sometimes when we are in meditation, or in a deeply relaxed state, then the windows to our Angels are momentarily opened and a vision of an Angel can sometimes be seen. Angels often bring messages to us during our sleep. Angels are more often felt as a presence than actually seen as a vision.
If you see an Angel in your dream, then this is an Angelic sign that your requests have been heard from your heart. An Angel is with you. Just ask in your waking day for exactly what you need. Say *'Dear Angel, please can you help me to manifest my heart's desires which are.......'* (Remember to speak from your heart). Thank your Angel.

Number plates

Angels can give you a sign in many forms and often use number plates to let you know that they have heard you. I asked if someone who was close to me would be ok in the Afghanistan war. I was driving at the time but this thought had come into my mind. The next two cars that came towards me had the following number plates…. WAR and 5AFE (safe). The next time you make a request to the Angels, don't forget to look at number plates on your next journey.

A Divine Moment

In a moment life can change
In a moment the dark becomes the light

In one moment there can be a profound experience
In one moment there can be realisation, as the soul opens to the love of the Angels
In a moment, a Divine Moment!

How to recognise the words of an Angel

When an Angel talks to you, the message will always be relayed from a position of love and peace. Your Angel will guide you towards loving resolutions, not only for yourself, but also for others.

- An Angel will speak directly about you, *'Michelle, you are very loved. You are a beacon of Light'*
- An Angel will allow you free will to make your own choices
- An Angel will always feel loving, nurturing and peaceful
- An Angel will always advise for the highest good of all concerned
- An Angel will instil calm and reassurance that the Universe is always protecting you
- An Angel's presence will be gentle, non-threatening, wise and all encompassing

'Dear Ones, this is your Angel. We only speak of love, wisdom and peace. Our main aim is only to provide and support you with unconditional love'.

Am I hearing my Ego or the Angels?

The ego is fear, Angels are love. To discern whether you are hearing your ego or your Angel then you need to ask *'Are the things that I am hearing or feeling, coming from a place of love or fear'?* The Angels will only know how to answer your prayers from love. Ask the Angels to show you a sign to validate their presence.

Angels Rejoice

Angels rejoice when we reach our hand out to them. You are warmly welcomed into the abode of the Angels heart. You will know this, because you will feel an overwhelming sense of peace and calm. You will have a moment of knowing, a divine and profound moment.

Reach out to your Angel today and feel your life change. You will experience a miracle as you are accepted and nurtured. To know an Angel is to know profound Bliss

How do I open my Heart

To open your Heart
Just ask the Angels to be with you
Ask the Angels to help you experience a Divine Moment
The Angels will hear you
Your Divine Moment will come
A profound experience, life changing......

Synchronicity or coincidence?

Synchronicity is the meeting of two paths. They meet at the exact moment that is beneficial to both parties, to both purposes, to both souls.

- We ask for guidance from our soul and the teacher or the lesson appears
- We ask for love and the lover of the lesson about loving ourselves appears
- We ask about life and our path and Divine purpose become apparent

Nothing is ever a coincidence, everything is always exactly as you requested at a soul level or thought level. Everything appears with Divine timing.

Everything and everyone that comes into our life is a lesson or a gift. If you are wise they are both. When we begin to call upon our Angels, then one sign that the Angels use to show us their presence, is through synchronicity.

Manifestation

Angels see your life from a higher perspective, they see the overall plan. Do no limit your perspective, on what can be achieved, when you work with trust and believe in your Angels.

Where there are Angels
Miracles can and do happen

Thank your Angels, go about your day. Release your requests fully to the Angelic realms, they will manifest, with Divine timing. Your Angels will leave you signs to show you that they have heard you, while you are waiting.

Why can't all people see Angels?

Just as each of us is individual, so is the experience for each of us when we invite Angels into our lives. Angels come to us in a manner or form that we will best understand based on our level of spiritual understanding and our level of peace and love.

Some people see, some people hear, some people sense, some people know. These are all ways of understanding our Angels.

If you want to see your Angel look at your life in more detail, more slowly, more deliberately. When you call an Angel, you will receive a sign or synchronicity. The signs or synchronicities will only have deep meaning or relevance for you.

Be open to seeing the signs from your Angel and the evidence of seeing, hearing, feeling and knowing will become bountiful gifts. The more you train your senses to be in the moment, the more you allow yourself to become calm and peaceful.

The more you simplify your life, releasing the dramas, and the attachments, then the clearer the existence of your Angels will be!

An Angel at the stream

A stream tinkles past in the sunlight and among the green leaves I hear birdsong
Beneath my feet I feel the softness of the fresh green grass
And I breathe in the sweetness, the purity and the essence of all this natural world
As the rising mist is released by the warmth of the morning sun, a formation can be seen all around me like giant wings, the beauty enfolds me.
In that Divine moment my Angel reaches out and touches me

Her essence is in my hair
Her sound is in my ears
Her love is in my heart

The love of my Angel is everywhere. In nature it is in all places, all sights, all smells and all sounds. Whilst on a craggy rock, take a moment. In that moment you experience the meaning of everything!

An Angels Song

An Angel's song is sublime
The notes create heavenly magic
As we sleep, the serenading protects and soothes our soul and our ethereal bodies
Every note, a healing vibration
Every song, a healing anthem
Every concert, a healing miracle!

Angels sing over us as we sleep

What does an Angel see when he looks at me?

What does an Angel see
When he looks at me?

What does an Angel feel
When he embraces me?

What does an Angel hear
When he speaks to me?

What does an Angel think
When he is walking, protecting and guiding me?

'I wish my Angel could tell me these things, then I could understand and feel closer. Angel, please leave me a sign which answers how you feel about my progress today'

Be open to your sign. An Angel always answers any request which is made with good intention, from an open heart.

Angels will leave you a sign, you only have to ASK!

The Angels are in the air that you breath

The Angels are in the air that you breath
The light of the sun
The sound of the wind
The beat of your heart

Your Angels are with you in each and every moment. To draw your Angels close to your heart be in your peace. Still your mind and feel the Angels touching your heart today.

A peaceful heart is a healing heart
Where there is a healing heart, there are Angels!

Angel Sign Experiences

How can I know the signs from my Angels?

How can I know the sings from my Angels we have two of them right will you let me know what to look for, please much love to ya.

Hello, if you have been asking your Angels specifically for help then you will receive a sign that is important to you, in a place or situation where only you will understand the meaning. Maybe the words of a song on the radio, or a truck with a name on the side, a car number plate, a feeling of peace coming over you. There are many signs.

The starting point is to follow the instructions for getting to know your Guardian Angel, get to know how your Guardian Angel feels, smells, sounds, looks, what is your Guardian Angels name? If you build up the connection with your Guardian Angel by speaking regularly, then you will understand your signs of their presence. Write everything in your Angel Journal. Blessings Michelle

Angels speak to you through your heart – Archangel Chamuel

Hello Michelle, I have two confronted views... one that says that everything is consciousness and there is only it and the other that everything is full of magic... but people who see the first, says that they don't experience the subtle realities.

When we engage with the Angelic realms, we are in our state of bliss. Our consciousness is expanded, it becomes finer and purer and lighter. Our ego is released and in that moment the reality of love, profound love can reach us. These feelings are so profound, all encompassing, healing and uplifting that we experience them as feelings of euphoria or magic. This is not our imagination; this is our heart recognising the vibrations and sounds of those that love us eternally and unconditionally. It is the recognition of our Angels.

Earthly matter and structures do not exist in the Angelic realms, only blissful feelings of freedom and space. There is no time, no limitations, and no ego. The mind is a powerful tool but do not let it hinder the messages, feelings and emotions of your heart. The Angels speak to you through your heart Dear One. Your intuition is your Angel. If your heart feels like this is magical, accept it! Nothing is in the imagination when it is felt by the heart. Allow your heart to guide you eternally.
Archangel Chamuel

Two Angels were beside my bed

I'm not new to this page but I've never said "hello". I have received two angel feathers just this year. The second one appeared when I was reading my Bible and saw something from the corner of my eye. It was the smallest of feathers just sticking out of my shirt on my arm.

I have also seen 2 angels beside my bed. The first one startled me when I awoke and saw a white figure bending over me. When I awakened fully, I realized what I had seen. I talk to my angels all the time. God and the angels comfort me and I feel blessed.

Hello, how lovely to meet you here today. Yes the vision of Angels is so profound and life changing it is hard to describe, but it is never forgotten.

The feathers are indeed your on-going sign that they are still there with you. Your belief and trust helps them to stay close at all times. Blessings to you dear one. Michelle

Angel Clouds spelled out the name of my Grandmother

Hello Michelle, 15 months ago I sat in a park reading a book (ironically about Angel messages). I had wished so much for a message, yet never expected anything.

After a sitting there for a few minutes I gazed up at the sky, which was a really bright azure blue & totally clear but to my absolute surprise there were 3 huge letters written in cloud so precisely above me spelling the name ENA...

As uncontrollable tears rolled down my cheeks as I scrambled to take my mobile phone from my bag to capture this remarkable sight, the letters faded & dissolved & sadly, I was unable to capture a photo.

ENA is the name of my Grandmother who raised me, she passed over in 1978. The letters were even in her handwriting. I will never forget this special sight as long as I live.

I am hoping you may have you heard of this before? I am careful who I tell for fear of being disbelieved. Very close friends & some family members understand I was desperate to get a witness but strangely there wasn't a soul in sight to witness this. Yet the letters were bigger than several jumbo jets together! Hopefully you may be familiar with similar happenings, I really hope so.

A close friend of mine had at teenage nephew who died & whilst his parents were abroad on holiday they both witnessed writing in cloud across a clear blue Spanish sky...It spelled 'Love Forever'....   Their son's photograph was displayed back home within a frame baring the words 'Love Forever' luckily they captured it & sent it to a magazine which printed it. I cried when I read the article, because it became my 'proof' that Yes, this does happen. Thank You for your time, Love, Peace & Blessings

Wow, what two beautiful signs from the Angels. They truly can give us such magic sometimes. What a profound experience to receive an Angel message from your Grandmother in the clouds. Thank you so much for sharing these two wonderful experiences. Blessings as always, Michelle

My son passed away .... I asked for a sign......

After my son recently passed away, I asked him for a sign. I needed to know that his spirit continued to live and was with me at times. That morning there were occurrences, but I wasn't quite sure if I was reading something into them that really weren't from him. So I asked him for a sign that was unquestionably from him. Later that morning a car turned ahead of me, it had a license plate that said, "A SIGN". Clear enough! Right?

Hello , yes that was your sign, loud and clear. Sorry to hear about the loss of your son but the Angels had heard you and sent you a sign. The sign was to show you that your son is always with you. The bonds of love are eternal. Ask Archangel Azrael to be with you. He will help you to work through the different stages of grief. Blessings Michelle

Small white Butterfly, sent by my Angel in heaven

Hi Michelle, My Sister passed at 212am on the 22 July 2012. My Sister passed unexpectedly after being on life support for a week. We got to say good bye but my life will never be the same. My strong spiritual beliefs have helped me through this very tough time. My sister was the main carer for our father who is in aged care. I live 16 hours' drive away and am now sharing the care with my other sister who lives a further 10 hours away. As you can imagine the are quite a few hurdles.

Not long after she passed I had a reading and was told that my sister is always with me and that whenever I see a small white butterfly that is her making her presence known. I never realised how comforting seeing a small white butterfly. Caring for our father I often have to make phone calls, when I am at work I go to the lunch room and look at the window. I work in the city on the 9th floor. Whenever I have phone calls especially the difficult ones I always look out the window and I always see a small white butterfly. I know my sister is with me guiding me, helping me to make the right choices and she calms me. It gives me such peace and strength. I know she is near and she is at peace too. Yes I always acknowledge her when I see a small white butterfly and just thinking of her helps me to overcome any struggle.

Michelle I know this sound strange but so many wonderful things have happened to me and I have found such peace that I know my angel in *heaven is always with me and she looks after me always. Thank you for the opportunity to share.*

Hello Dear Heart, nothing you have said to me here is at all strange. In fact, I am very glad that you have been able to have such a wonderful and loving experience. This is another fantastic way that the Angels can use to bring to us signs from our departed loved ones.

The peace that you feel is a sign that they have heard your requests and in that moment they are bringing you the peace that you need. Seeing the little white butterfly brings you such a wonderful profound feeling. This is of course also helping you to heal from your loss.
Thank you so much for sharing this very moving story. Blessings as always, precious girl. Michelle

If I smell cigarette smoke is that my Angel?

When i smell cigarette smoke in the house (my mother was a smoker) does that mean my mother is right next to me? Or when just half of my body gets wicked chills for a few seconds does that mean an angel is near me?

Hello, the sensations you describe are the sensations of spirit, not Angels. Angels are more ethereal and so their sensations will be subtle, for instance the smell may be of flowers, or angelic scent. The feelings are of a very light touch, ethereal touch. Please follow the meditation how to meet your Guardian Angel and you will start to recognise the touch of your Guardian Angel. You may also discover his or her name. Let me know how you get along. Blessings Michelle

I want to share something

I am from India today is Saturday 2nd February 2013, when last night i was sleeping and i saw one dream in that dream there were so many white feathers in front of me, i picked up 1-2 feathers and put it into my shirt pocket. when i woke up i realized oh..it was my dream. but felt that maybe Angel was closed to me at that time..so i saw that dream..
Have A wonderful week end. Thank you Amen :-)

Hello, beautiful dream. This was your sign that your Angels are indeed close to you and hearing you. Enjoy this moment of increased spiritual awareness now, as you journey with your Angels. Blessings Michelle

---

Choirs of Angels/Angel Music

I have had a wonderful experience I was woken up by the sound of beautiful music. I sat up in the bed looked around for the source but it was coming from above me. I asked out loud 'what is this I am hearing'? A voice answered 'you are listening to the choir of Angels'.
It stirred my husband awake 'who are you talking to he asked'? 'Shush'! I said, as I placed my hand on his chest 'the Angels are here' . He drifted back to a peaceful sleep. I relaxed back listening to the gentle angelic sounds. I thanked the Angels for allowing me to hear them. They must have sung me back to sleep. When I woke again I was so happy in myself.

Angels love to sing! What a wonderful and profound experience. I have also had the experience of hearing Angelic music.

Angel Aroma

This morning I was woken by this strong beautiful smell.... as I was awakening I was thinking .... 'wow that new washing powder smells so nice'!.... then I realised that it was in fact the aroma of my Angels as I sleep on the third floor of my house, and the washing was in the machine!.... My mother died on the 27th December 2012 and I think this was my sign today.... as was the feather that floated in front of me during my dog walk on that same day.

Angel Gift

My best friend made me an angel guide stone for Christmas along with a single jingle bell. The stone has an angel on the front and the word "Guide" on the back. She told me I could pray on the stone to call on my

angels when I need help and guidance. She also told me to ring the jingle bell everywhere to get rid of negative energy, or to ring it when I need my angels, because angels love the sound of bells. I loved this gift. It really has helped me. I also but jingle bells on the door handles of my bedroom and in a couple other spots so that when I open the doors, in theory, I'm constantly clearing negative energy. I love this so much, I thought I would share it with you.

What a thoughtful gift from your friend. The Angels just love the sound of bells and they will indeed help to lift the energy in your home. Angels love to gather in homes that are filled with angelic sounds and the energies of peace and love.

I dreamt I was flying ......

I dreamed of flying a couple nights ago. So much fun BUT I wasn't sure how to land. :)

Hello, I asked about this for you in meditation. Flying in our dreams is a great blessing. It means that our souls are mature enough to see the Universal teachings for Humanity and beyond. Ask your Guardian Angels to fly with you and help your spirit body to re-enter your physical body in full alignment after you have seen your teachings for that day

Man at the church

I have been feeling down this year due to various issues... A man walked up to me after church service and told me that all will be alright. I don't know him from Adams. Never met him before. He told me he had lost everything due to spending all his waking hours making money, investing for his company & did very well for his firm & family but he felt he had lost what truly mattered in his life...

His own kids wouldn't even allow him to carry them or stay in the same room with him when they were growing up because they did not bond with him ..He was a stranger to his own family When he lost all his savings, & his job eventually, he told me that he found himself...

Then he thanked me for listening and walked away. I turned around & there was no one around me at all. He wanted me to know that all would be alright cos as he put it, I had too much on my mind & that they hear me..whatever he meant buy that!!!...I think he meant the Angels & saints...what do you think?

Hello I just love this story as it is a perfect example of how the Angels come to us in Human form in our time of need. If this is the way they can get a message to you most clearly then they appear in human form and the words resonate on a deep level.

I think this man was clearly saying to you that despite all your challenges, never forget the things that are truly important to you?

Thank you so much for sharing this with us. What a wonderful Angelic gift of wisdom that was imparted to you that day, something you can remember with fondness. Blessings Michelle

Saved from drowning by an Angel!

God has sent angels twice that I positively know of. I'm sure though, that in my life He has sent them so many times I cannot count! One time, I watched the sun set at Hollywood Beach, north side, by the pier. I got caught in a rip tide and was pulled out past the pier. I treaded water as long as I possibly could, hoping I would get out of the rip tide so I could then swim in. By this time it was dark and there was no one anywhere around. I knew I wouldn't be able to stay up much longer and it was so dark, I feared what may be swimming below me..and I knew I was definitely going to drown any time..I prayed and then prepared to just go ahead and take a deep breath of water to get it over with quickly....when all of a sudden out of the dark I was swooped out of the water and laid onto a surfboard. The man swam me to shore and walked me to the light where the pier meets the sand. I looked around to try to get my bearings..and in that short second..when I turned back to thank him..he was nowhere within sight. There was no one else around either. I know it was an angel sent to save me.

On the tree it said LOVE! - Nature Angels

I wanted to share something I encountered a few months ago. I was walking along the river where I live near with my dog. Was a normal day, on the way back from my walk there are trees everywhere which I'd pass every day.

However this particular day as I was walking I felt myself drawn to a force to glance and notice its coming from a tree. This sudden urge came over me to hug this tree, it was calling me, in search, and in response found its message embarked on the tree it's said "LOVE" right there in huge engraved letters I was so overwhelmed and started to tear.

I call it my "love tree" and hug it almost every day without fail I hug it and immediately feel calmness at peace. I'd like to know if You may explain to me what you believe this to be? Thank you!! :-))

Hello, you are an Angel of the Earth, also known as a light worker, and as such you feel things very acutely at all levels of existence. You were being a shown a sign, and the energy of the tree was calling you towards it. This would of been orchestrated by the Nature Angels who reside outside and would of been wanting to give you this message on that day. What a lovely gift from your Angels dear one. Thank you for sharing your lovely story. Blessings Michelle

I saw a vision of my Guardian Angel

Thank you Michelle and Blessings to you for sharing all that you do with our Angels.

What is amazing, which I'd like to share and let others know....is that my Guardian Angel showed herself to me while I was having a vision of my past home I grew up in, which was encased in all darkness, she showed me

that she was really there all along watching over me above that darkness.

That WAS a profound moment to know I was not alone in all that I went through during that time of my life. Again, Blessings to you Michelle.

Hello, what a wonderful vision from your Angel showing you how much you have always been protected and this will continue. I understand what you say when you say about the moment being profound. This is absolutely true. When we meet our Angels there is nothing that ever can compare. Thank you so much for sharing your story. Blessings dear one. Michelle

I need help ......I need a sign

Hello Michelle, I am going through a particularly bad period at the moment and I have always believed in angels, I have never had an encounter or anything I just believe...I am having a hard time now though even meditating. I beg for any kind of sign and even speak directly to The archangel Michael...but nothing. Any suggestions? I could really use the help.....Thank you.

Hello, What I always suggest is for you to:

- take a quiet time, where you can feel peaceful and calm
- take your Angel Journal and just write
- Write everything about how you feel in your heart
- Write everything, as if you were telling your most trusted friend, you can say anything and everything
- Now ask the Angels to help you find solutions, healing and answers.......

The Angels will help you, and they will find you solutions. Say **'May this or something greater now manifest for the greatest good of all concerned'. Now ask the Angels to send some help or healing to someone else who may benefit from a sign or some love from their Angel.** Thank the **Angels.**

Put your journal away and go about your day feeling confident in the knowledge that you will now see synchronicities, or signs from your Angels. Keep reading all the posts on how to write to and to know your **Guardian Angel** and everyday try to find a regular time to talk to, think about or speak about your **Angels**. **Write** everything every day in your **Journal**. Over time you will look back and see how many answers and solutions have been provided for you. Just **Ask, Trust, and Believe**. Blessings dear one. Michelle

---

I don't feel, see or know anything…..

20 years ago I was shown my future by two angels…they showed me places and situations that I should be prepared for and perhaps try to remember so that I would have the strength to stand up… I've seen things known things and believed all my life, but sometimes I just fall to the ground and just don't feel, see or know anything…

Hello, what a profound and life changing experience. Sometimes, the feeling of being on the ground as you describe, is another way for the Angels to show you your own strength. It is in the experience of getting back on our feet that we learn. This is a sign of your spiritual maturity, where the Angels step back and allow you to find your own way for a little while. They do this as a way for you to learn more deeply about your own strength and wisdom. The Angels are always with you watching you, sending you love and protecting you. You have just forgotten in that moment to call them. Remember to ask them to draw closer if you ever feel that you need their support and most importantly, don't forget to thank them. Blessings Dear One Michelle

How do I know it is an Angel's sign and not just wishful thinking?

I am very New to communicating with my Angels. I have had a numerous things happen since then to show me they love me an want to help. The very big one was letting go of a past love. I asked for help and received it. I began to work hard to put him behind me. But still he lingers. I asked my Angels for clues as to if I should be letting it go. I feel like they really want to tell me No.. I have had passages opened to me from Matthew. I have had Angel saying things like if it's in your heart everyday maybe you should not let it go. **How do I look for signs Angels are telling me and not my wish-full thinking. Thanks for the help. Love and Blessings to you?**

Angels talk to our hearts through our intuition, if you are following a path based on **love and not from fear**, then you are usually on the right track.

The **Angels** will give you a sign to show you. **There are no mistakes, only learning's.** If you make a decision and then find that you need to go another way, the **Angels** are with you to support and love you unconditionally.

Angels allow you **free will** and will never tell you what to do. Instead, they will gently show you when you are on the right track. **Listen to your heart.**

Ask the **Angels** to show you **discernment** when choosing a partner
Ask the **Angels** to **let go** of situations that no longer serve you
Ask the **Angels** to help you **forgive** not just others but also yourself for things you perceive you have done incorrectly

Angels are waiting to help you with everything, they rejoice when you are happy, and joyful.
Make an **Angel** happy today, do what your **heart desires!** Blessings as always, Michelle

Heavenly sign from my cat

When I lost my Tangie after 17 yrs to brain cancer, I was so devastated.. I felt so lost without him and w/o his constant love/companionship. Then one night I had a dream of him watching me with a black cat snuggling next to me. I felt such peace like it was ok to move on. We ended up adopting a black cat (which I didn't go looking for at first) and ironically, the name the shelter gave her was....ANGELICA! I knew then she was sent to me! I still miss Tangie, but know I'll see him again someday.

Animals stay by our side even when they pass to another dimension. They are always with us. Thank you for your lovely story about Tangie and Angelica. Blessings as always. Michelle

Response

That's what I like to believe too. Even on the day we were bringing Angelica home, I asked Tangie to watch over her. I think he knew it would be ok. I just couldn't believe when we went looking and my son saw her first. He said, "look mom, her name is Angelica!" Knowing I love angels and collect them, it just brought it all together. :)

Angels sent me a sign – a heart shaped…

One day last week as I was walking up the sidewalk to work, I always think of my angels guiding me as I am partially disabled and depend on my cane as well. As I was just thinking of angel feathers, about 2 feet ahead of me, I saw a heart shaped object. It was a beautiful yellow leaf in the perfect shape of a heart! I unfortunately was unable to reach it to pick it up, but it sure was reassuring that my angels surround me at all times

That is a wonderful sign to receive from your Angels. I am going to repost this for all to see. Thank you for sharing. Blessings Michelle

Church Bells

As I walked on my way to Diagnostic Imaging Center to have my test done early this afternoon, it was bright and sunny with cool Autumn breeze blew against my face and I heard a beautiful faint sound of church bells coming from afar. That made me realized, perhaps my Angel was telling me and giving me a sign that I will be alright. I had the result back, the tumour didn't change in size and it remained benign.

What beautiful signs to receive from your Angels. Thank you so much for sharing your experience and I am so happy that your tumour was found to be benign. If you continue to now work with the Angels of healing and Archangel Raphael this will keep your health topped up and vibrant. Blessings to you dear one, Michelle

Angel shell, feather and worry stone, when my husband passed away

Here's an odd story for all. My husband passed away this last April. I was devastated that I had to travel 2300 miles back home.

My first camping trip I was walking in the river and I was meditating and crying because I missed him and was saddened by the fact that he wasn't there with me to witness the beauty of the river and everything around me at the time.

While I was crying and missing him a blue Jays feather flowed right in front of me. I picked it up and started walking towards the shore.

On the shore where I walked up another blue black and white blue jays feather was in my path. It was resting in an angel wing shell with a round rock that was smooth like it had been someone's worry stone and rubbed smooth over the years. This was resting on top of the feather in the angel wing shell. To this day I still have all of them.

Hello, I was so moved by this story of how the Angels managed to get a message to you in such a beautiful way. It would be lovely if you could post a photo if you have one. I would love to see your beautiful blue black and white jays feathers this must of really helped you to heal some of your grief after the loss of your husband. You can also call upon Archangel Azrael for help with working through the various stages of loss and grief.

Thank you for sharing your lovely story. I feel you husbands gentle presence around you.
Blessings Michelle

Call your Angels, witness Miracles

I firmly believe in angels.. I had a problem which i could never see being solved. I prayed to Gabrielle Michael plus my own guardian angel whom i call "Grace" the name came to me as my angel. So i am happy to have her with me each day. My problem solved and i was so lucky. It had resolved b4 i even knew it....

Hello, I totally understand this sort of miracle. Whenever we believe and work with our Angels, things miraculously start to fall into place. Thank you for sharing you experience with us. Hope to hear from you often.
Blessings Michelle

Response: *Thank you.. I am very happy to share this story. I always think of angels daily. They bring so much peace within one. Yes this problem i had just fell into place nicely.. I was so touched. I read a lot of angel books. And you know they bring so much happiness to people worldwide. Amazing the connection people have with angels.......♥ ♥*

I have stopped wondering, asking, worrying about everyday things

Thought I'd pop in send my blessing for a beautiful evening and to say since joining your page and reading when I'm on Facebook your posts it's been about a month that I have started to just simply say THANK YOU apart from my love tree that I had written to you about and knowing I'm from a higher power and all the things around me are that from angels, I have stopped wondering, asking, worrying about the everyday things, the ifs, the buts, and so forth, I simply say THANK YOU to my lord my angels knowing that all I ask want need will come! And yes you've guessed it they are all coming at the right moments and I'm so grateful. My angels soothe me! They comfort me! I'm not aware of my future and what tomorrow brings but I'm in peace bcos the angels are guiding me and all bcos im wholeheartedly saying THANK YOU. So thank you also to this page as it's from all your posts and readings I've learnt this lesson! In all that happens in life give thanks! Blessing to you all ☺x

Hello, what lovely news. I am so glad that you have managed to connect with your Angels and you are learning from them how to be in your peace and just go with the flow. What a wonderful time for you in your life. Remember, to write everything down in your Angelic Journal to remind you how far you have come. Thank you for sharing your experiences with us. Blessings as always dear one. Michelle

The Angels left feathers under the children's nightlight

Hi Michelle. My Angel calling cards I find are feathers in impossible places. In times when I am under stress. This may sound bizarre. When my husband died I thought my world had ended. Was 23 years old with 2 small kids. I was sitting outside when a dove landed on my head! It just sat there. I dozed off outside with the dove still on my head. When I woke up again the dove was gone. Later I found 3 perfect dove feathers on my children's night stand, neatly tucked just under their nightlight. Over the following days leading up to the funeral I found more feathers in the house. At the funeral a dove landed on the casket and sat there until the casket started to descend into the grave. I remember someone asking if the bird was ill. I said 'no, it is my Angel'. My children now grown and have begun their own families also still find 'calling cards'.. Uriel was letting me know that all would be ok and we are never alone!

What do number synchronicities mean like 11.11, 12.12?

What do number synchronicities mean like 11.11, 12.12?

Number synchronicities are the awakening codes for energies and crystals in and around the Universe. They will be synchronised and activated at a precise moment in time. A time which has previously been agreed by Divine Will. Angels support this ascension of the planet. The number synchronicities are a sign of their presence during these energetic changes.

I believe in Angels

I believe in Angels because 41 yrs. ago I had an out of body experience, a beautiful tall Angel came and took me to the presence of Jesus. Jesus asked me " what have you done for me?, I said, "I have Loved you very much and I have tried to serve you." "I know he said, It's not your time yet, go back, I will answer a prayer you have always asked of me." I knew what that prayer was - that my husband become a Christian. March 14, 2012 my husband Moses died, but a week before he died he repented and accepted the Lord. The Lord reminded me of the out of body experience and the promise he made to me that he would ans. my prayer.

What a beautiful experience.... I myself believe greatly in the power of prayer and have been lucky to know the presence of Jesus. Angelic signs and visions are usually presented to us in a way that we can personally comprehend. There is no doubting this wonderful sign that you received. If you speak to the Angels now about Moses, you will again be sent another sign by your Angels that he is very happy and indeed still with you. The bonds of love made from our hearts are eternal. Thank you for sharing your profound experience. Blessings dear one. Michelle

What does a Black Angel mean?

Maybe you could help? I had a dream about a black winged angel putting his fist straight through my chest where my heart is, and I woke up, my heart pounding. I usually forget my dreams immediately but not this one. Maybe you can shed some light on this.

The Black Angel is a deep rooted fear, maybe from your past life or from teachings in your childhood about religion. Your subconscious sees religion as having good and bad, light and dark, Angels and demons but in reality there is only love!
You have created a deep fear sub-consciously that something, not of the light, could take your heart.
- Ask Archangel Michael to be with you now
- Ask him to walk with you
- Ask him to cut the cords of sub-conscious programming about religion or doctrine that no longer serve you
- Ask that he bathe you in his light of healing and protection

If you do not know the presence of your Guardian Angel, then make time to meditate and start to work on drawing her near to you. She will love and protect you always!

You can call Archangel Michael when you are dreaming and he will come. Say *'Archangel Michael, be with me now!* You are always safe and protected in the light of your Angels!

Angel asks directions for the Church

Must tell you this story.... Years ago when I was picking my children up from the bus stop after school.... There was this little plump lady very scruffy no teeth hair looked lit it had never been combed and had an old bag of stuff she had picked out of a bind by the looks of it and smell.... She asked me if I could take her to the Catholic church which was in the opposite direction I was going... but I said 'yes'. Well my children blocked their noses as she smelt like urine and alcohol and body odour.... She talked of seeing the Priest at the church and said she knew him... we finally got there and she got out and walked to the church... and she just disappear like she was poof gone.. was she an Angel??? I knew the Priest at this church they didn't know or see this little old lady... I believe she was an Angel so we never know who we may be helping ... strange.

My Angel drove me to the hospital

My Angel Experience. We pulled into the parking lot and found a place to unload the bike. My husband, David, came around to help me but I waived him off. I knew it would take me a while to get out and I didn't want to be rushed. He went to the back of the car and tugged at the bike rack. I heard the bike tires hit the pavement. I struggled to get out of the car – first bracing myself and then pulling on the top of the car door. At eight months pregnant, a bicycle race in the heat of the summer would make for a long day.

We had driven for three hours on two-lane roads, through farming areas and small towns to reach our destination in a rural area outside of Athens, Georgia. Hundreds of cyclists were gathered for a large regional race. I found a shady spot under a tree and unfolded my chair. I had a bag of books and I planned to read most of the day. I kissed David as he left to join the pack of people getting their numbers pinned on and lining up for the race. I sat down and tried to get comfortable. I rubbed my stomach and comforted my squirmy, unborn girl, Megan. I told her it would be a while before her dad came back and she needed to settle down.
About 45 minutes into the race, I lowered my sunglasses to watch the other spectators milling around. Something was going on. They were

talking to each other and hurriedly packing their cars and scrambling around leaving. I watched as an older man in bicycle shorts walked toward me with a mangled bicycle. As he got closer I could tell it was David's bike. I sat up and pushed with both arms to stand and meet him.

He told me that thirty cyclists went down on a curve and a dozen or more are on their way to St. Mary's hospital in Athens with road burn and broken bones. They thought David had a broken leg. He helped me load the bike in the car and gave me directions to the hospital.
He strapped the parts of the bike that were still intact onto the back of the car and stuffed the loose and broken parts into the back seat. My mind was racing as he gave me directions to the hospital.
Highway what? Turn where? I wasn't familiar with the area and his directions weren't making sense. He said the hospital was about an hour away. He turned to go help another family and left me standing beside the car. Cars were streaming out of every exit of the field as people headed out to the hospital. As I turned to face the car it occurred to me that we had driven up in David's car: a straight shift and I didn't know how to drive it. Now was NOT the time to learn.

My legs started to shake and my heart was pounding in my ears. I felt like I was going to pass out. I was overwhelmed and I couldn't think straight. I didn't know how I'd ever find the hospital. I could feel panic welling up inside of me.

The doctor said I could travel if I'd be careful and take care of myself. I held my protruding stomach "Don't worry Megan – we'll be alright. Everything will be fine." I tried to reassure myself but the panic was mounting. I took several deep breaths and tried to gather my thoughts. I felt tears come to my eyes and stream down my face. My hands were trembling. I began to pray.

I sensed someone approaching and turned to see a beautiful blond girl. She said "Hi, my name is Megan. Both of my parents are on their way to the hospital and you look like you could use some help." I broke down crying, relieved that someone was offering help. I explained the circumstances to her and she helped me into the passenger seat. As we settled in to the ride she explained that she was 15 years old but her birthday was only a month away, on July 25th. She said her dad had taught her to drive a straight shift. He was a cyclist that had been injured and he was on his way to the hospital as well. In a soothing tone she assured me that she was a good driver and knew exactly where she was going. We made small talk and she smiled when I told her my due date was mid-July and that I'd already decided on Megan as my baby's name. Time passed quickly and before I knew it we were at the hospital.

Megan whipped the car into a parking space near the hospital entrance. She stretched out her hand to give me the keys. Her face had the serenity of an angel. She took both of my hands tightly in hers and said. "Don't worry. He's OK. Everything is going to be alright."
Several nuns, realizing that I was hugely pregnant, swarmed me excitedly and took me into the hospital. As I looked back to thank Megan – she was already gone. The nuns realized that I wasn't in labour but they put me in a wheelchair anyway. They pushed me down to where David was laying on a gurney having his wounds treated. He said "Don't worry honey. My leg is not broken. I've just got really bad road burn".

After a short stay in the hospital David was able to drive back to Macon. As we settled back into our routine, I often thought of the young woman that was so kind to me at such a difficult time.

My daughter, Megan, was born on July 25th.

I've thought back to that day many times. Her name was Megan, her birthday was July 25th. Why would a 15 year old girl's parents let her drive a woman she didn't know to a hospital an hour away? Where was her mom? Her dad was hurt and on his way to the hospital. He taught her to drive a straight shift. The only conclusion is that God loaned me an Angel. The Megan of the future came down for a couple of hours to help us through a crisis. I thought of putting an ad in the newspaper to try to find her, but the more I think about it – the more I'm certain that I wouldn't be able to find her. She was my Angel on Loan.

Feathers in my kitchen

Hello! Everyone , I want to share something with you yesterday when i was coming out from Gym and i was on the road at that time i just felt that how life is beautiful, at that time one white feather fell in front of me then suddenly i realized that may be it was Angel near to me how beautiful experience it was isn't it? I didn't pick up that White feather but when i came to my home i found one small white and black feather in my kitchen and i kept it into my Angel feather box...:-)

Specially Thanx to Michelle for creating this page and i learned a lot about Angels from Michelle. Thank you dear Michelle may God bless you :-)

Hello, I have a big smile for your happiness after finding your precious Angel signs. Blessings as always Michelle

My Angel Sign

I never really find feathers, but I have a Hibiscus scented candle on my altar and throughout the day during what seem like random moments, I am overwhelmed with the scent. I have even asked those around me if they can smell it? It took a while before I recognised the scent, but now I know it is a sign from my Angels.

I thought meeting Angels was impossible, until I met them!

May I take this opportunity to thank you for giving me the knowledge and the inspiration to connect with the angels. I kind of thought it was bullshit (sorry) until I met them lol. They communicate to me all the time through music (usually when I am driving too fast, I will hear a STOP, or SLOW DOWN, but there are many other ways they make themselves known to me, and I celebrate it! Family and friends say 'co-incidence' but no way! It can be a battle to communicate though, sometimes I don't get their name, the message comes through too fast. I ask them to slow down so that I may understand, but I think they might be from Glasgow, because they won't slow down or repeat lol. So glad to be on touch with this Divine Gift, it is so reassuring.

Hello, I have read your progress and you have made me laugh at your funny humour and also smile at the knowledge that you are getting to know your Angels. The most important thing I can say to you at this point is to just keep relaxing in your sanctuary and really take some quality time to know your Guardian Angel. She will be much more clear in her approach, more so than some of the more playful Angels. This will also help you to maintain the finer vibration needed to sustain a link with the Angelic realms. Thank you so much for letting us all know how you are getting along. Don't forget to thank your Angels and to write everything down in your Angelic Journal. Please keep letting me know how you get along and of course I will help you in any way that I can. What a great start to my day to hear about your progress! Blessings dear one. Michelle

Angels are something you think of when it is Christmas

Angels are something you think of when its Christmas, when I pray, I usually pray to God. I came across your page through a very dear friend of mine who for me is like an Angel. I enjoy reading your posts and I recall one post where you said that if you wanted to ask your Guardian Angel something we should ASK them to help with something. The thing is one of my son's friends is in hospital awaiting the result of a test he had done which we were very worried that it would come out positive and he is only a teenager. The thing is I came across your page last week and remembering your post I prayed every day to my guardian angel and asked him/her to please help him and his family overcome the battle they are faced with. Well today we called to them to see if they knew the results and it is NEGATIVE! You cannot believe how happy we are. He has to have an operation sometime next week but just knowing that it's negative is just awesome, so I am now praying and asking my guardian angel and God to be with him and help him get a speedy recovery. Thank you for your page and I just wanted to share this story with all your readers. Xoxoxox

Hello, how lovely to hear from you today and what wonderful news for your friend's son. Angels are messengers of your God and because of your intention and love within your heart when you asked for help, then help was provided. Remember to thank your Angels, they are Gods helpers and love being asked by you for help, this is their job.

Ask Archangel Raphael, the master healer to be with the teenager during his operation. When you pray and talk to your Angels you will begin to see more and more signs and synchronicities around you. Thank you for telling us your story. Blessings dear one. Michelle

Robins

The day after my little dog passed away, one by one robins gathered in the tree in my backyard...until there were 24 of them! It happened when I phoned my ex to tell him that she was gone.

Hello, I just love it when the Robins come to show me a sign.... it is very special and meaningful... 24 robins must have been very profound for you.... beautiful experience. Thank you for sharing, we are all learning together. Blessings as always, Michelle

Angels speak to us, through messages from strangers

The first ones I was made aware of were the random comments from strangers that seemed the perfect answer to my question that I didn't speak. For Example, one day I was working in Brampton, and I went into the bank to deposit my check, which was not quite enough to cover my expenses. A lovely woman looked right at me and said "Don't worry child, everything will be taken care of." And then when I went to the bank teller, she told me that I had $500.00 released from being on hold so that my expenses would be covered. Through conversations and research I have come to learn that angels do embody people to convey messages, just like

this one. And once you are aware of it, they usually find other ways to communicate (they moved to my dreams after I was aware)
But I have dozens more angel stories...I hear them daily, they tell me things to share with my clients during their massage treatments, they have me post things on FB and had me create 3 pages to share these messages. I do love the angels - and I know they love me too.

Section 7

Angel Feathers

Angel Feathers

If you find a fresh white feather, feel very blessed. This is a sign that your Angels have heard your prayers and that the manifestation of your hearts desires are being taken to the heart of God.

Keep the feather by your bed, or on your Angel altar. Thank the Angels. Go about your day. Feathers are a 'blessed' gift from your Angels. Cherish them, your blessings are about to arrive.

I have found a feather!

Pick up your feather today and hold it in your hand with pride
This is the most precious gift you will ever have bestowed upon you.
Within this gift is the meaning of life Unconditional Love from Heaven

---

The Colours of Feathers

If you receive a delicate or fresh feather, even if it is a different colour to white, then know that this is symbolic of the soul message you currently need to hear!

Pure White

Your pure requests to the Angels have been heard and Angels are with you

Pink

You are opening to the pink of unconditional love either by giving or receiving. You are learning that it is important to do both in equal measure

Red

Follow your passion with focus and determination. It is time to take action.

Yellow

If you find a yellow feather then this is a sign that you can feel 'joyful and optimistic'. Bright times are ahead. Embrace all opportunities as they are presented to you.

Brown

You are currently in need of grounding, and nurturing

Blue

In order to find your peace, then you may need to develop more clarity and focus in your communications.

Green

This is the colour of healing. The Angels have seen your need for emotional healing within your heart.

Orange

You are currently being shown that you have creative energy that has been recognised or is in need of being expressed.

Black/White

An indication to balance your male and female energies through the process of purification.

Grey

Grey feathers are a sign of ambiguity. A sign that you need to become clearer and more focused. It is time to sit down and set your intentions. It is from our intentions and our hearts desires that things manifest.

Black

Those things that have been troubling you will shortly have an answer. Call the Angels closer to help you gain clarity

Feather blowing in the wind

A feather blowing in the wind
A bird flying with its graceful wings
A dog jumping with its heart full of glee
Today is the day that the Angels want to speak

They speak with love, joy and passion, you can see it all around you, with every passing breeze or action

Open your eyes wide
See your Angels omnipresence and draw it deep inside
The Angels of love joy and peace always eternally by your side

Questions about Feathers

I have a black and white feather, what does it mean?

A black and white feather is an indication to balance all aspects all of ourselves. This includes balancing our conscious and subconscious selves, our inner qualities and all aspects of our male and female.

This may involve for example, looking at the aspects of your being that have become too controlling or rigid. You may like try to balance this control with more feminine aspects like nurture, compassion and intuition

If you already have well developed feminine qualities, then you may need to balance these with more clarity, focus or drive. These more direct qualities help you to complete things in your life and are the masculine aspects of your being.

The black and white feather is asking you to learn about all aspects of your anima and to work towards balance. This is part of your spiritual journey.

Balance male and female, through purification?

......Michelle ... What does it mean ...... balance male and female ..... through purification?
Michelle, what does it mean exactly when angels say balance your male and female energies through the process of purification? ♥

To balance your masculine and feminine energies means to release ego attached to either gender. To just embrace the present moment, from a position of complete surrender.

You allow all previous conditioning about men or women, to be released and you act from the love in your heart. The love in your heart is a perfect barometer of your progress on your spiritual path.

Ask the Angels, to bathe your heart in healing energy every moment, so that your spiritual compass, your heart, can be healed in all directions, all time frames and all life times.

The energies of male and female have been unbalanced on a Universal level, but now stronger 'Divine Feminine' energies are reaching many souls. This energy creates an 'awakening' so that the energy of male and female, yin and yang, can become balanced.

A balanced heart in one person, creates peace. Peace in one person radiates out and creates peace for others. Everything is interconnected

When one person finds peace
We all potentially find peace

Balance = Male and Female/Yin and Yang
Divine Feminine - the energy of healing from the dominance of male energies of ego. Release ego and balance is being restored

When my mother died ...... a story of feathers

When my mother passed away my sister and I slept in reclining chairs all night and awoke to white fluffy feathers everywhere, falling on us covering the floor and chairs.....it was the most beautiful site to this day we have no idea where they came from........ One thing I do know is Angels were with me, my mother and my sister. I carry some of the feathers with me to this day.

Small feather came flying out

i was taking cloths out of the dryer a little while ago and a very small feather came flying in front of me, i was so excited i let it land on my finger, then it flew up to the ceiling and disappeared it was beautiful, but so small, i feel blessed

I always think of the little feathers as a sign from the small playful giggling Angels. Thank you for sharing. Blessings Michelle

Multi-coloured feather, what does it mean?

Question: In your opinion, if one finds a multi-coloured feather is the message more from the spiritual message of the bird from where it came, all the colour meanings, or a combination?

For example, I have found over the past six months two flicker feathers which are brown, black, white, and orange. How would you interpret if you did not immediately receive an impression? Much gratitude for your thoughts

Hello this is a wonderful question. The colours on the feather are all showing you some message from your Angel about your journey. The more colours there are, the more things that are occurring for you at this time. At a quick glance I would say that you are in the process of balancing your yin and yang energy (your male and female aspects of self), this is the black and white. You are in need or grounding and nurturing (Brown). Then as part of this process your passion and creativity will begin to be expressed (Orange). So take care of you and your creativity and inspiration are ready to be brought forward. How exciting. Let me know how you get along. Blessings to you, Michelle

Fluffy Feather

Hi Michelle, Just wanted to share with u a beautiful image I'll never forget. I was driving last week, taking my daughter to school and from the middle

of nowhere in the middle of the car park, right in front of my car, a pure white fluffy feather was floating down like a huge snowflake. Put a smile on my face for the full day :-) x

Guardian Angel comforts me

Hello :) im new to this page i believe i have a few guardian angels looking over me at the moment.. lost a loved one and been finding feathers and feeling a presence

Hello, I am sorry to hear that you have recently lost a loved one. Please work with Archangel Azrael at this time, he will help you with all aspects of your grieving process. It is absolutely correct that your Guardian Angel will have drawn closer to you at this time, and the feather is your sign that the Angels are there to comfort you. All you have to do Dear One, is ask your Angels for what help you need. They are indeed waiting to reach out to you even more. Write everything in your Angelic Journal, this will help your connection and will also help you to heal your heart. Blessings to you as always precious lady. Michelle

How big does your feather have to be? I thought they were just from birds?

If you find a feather, what does it look like, will it be big or small. I thought all feathers were just from birds and that it was just wishful thinking on my part that I would actually get a sign from an Angel. I keep asking for a sign, but nothing yet. Maybe I am not a good enough person?

Everyone is worthy of receiving help and signs from the Angels. It is just learning to recognise how they work with your individually. A feather is normally clearly placed for you to see. It may be in your car, or it may float right in front of you, or land on your shoe or clothing! A feather is only one of the signs that an Angel may use if you have been asking for assistance. They use signs to show us that they have heard us and that answers are well and truly on their way.

The size of the feather is unimportant only that it is in a place that is significant for you. The Angels will use whatever materials they can find in this three dimensional earth and so your feather will no doubt have originated from a bird. It doesn't matter what size the feather is, more that, you recognise it as having been placed there specifically so that you would notice it.

Keep working on your vibration of peace and love, then the Angels will be able to draw ever more closely and will be able to leave you more signs of their presence in your daily life.

I still have not received my feather!

I still have never found my feather. I guess my aura must be black, so no Angels will give me one. I am hopeless?

The Angels will not be able to reach you unless you make your aura brighter with the belief and confidence that they are indeed with you.

Try to relax and follow the meditations on how to meet your Guardian Angel and practice regularly. Ask the Angels to give you a sign of their presence, a feather is only one of the ways that Angels use as they have many different ways of sending us a sign.

A feather is normally a sign that they are telling you that things are on track and that they have heard you and that they are with you. Learn all the ways an Angel can leave a sign and then train your senses to become more aware of those things happening in and around you, especially during meditation.

I was literally showered in white feathers

How wonderful . Thank you for sharing. Since my husband passed away in 2009 , this is the first year I am actually celebrating Christmas. I have long associated white feathers with angels & had many amazing experience with them appearing. When my husband was very ill I had a funeral to attend & was very anxious , on the day I was literally showered in white feathers in my garden. My neighbour even came to see what was happening, & we stood in awe of these feathers gently falling, the love & peace I felt was magnificent. Happily yesterday one appeared on my kitchen side . So I feel very comforted by that & will also cleanse as you suggested . I hope you don't mind me sharing this with you. Blessing's & love to you & thank you x

Hello I am so happy to hear that this year you will feel able to enjoy Christmas again. Your husband will be so pleased that you are once again starting to move forward in your life, and he supports this. I just love your wonderful and moving story about your husband and the wonderful feathers that the Angels used to give you a sign that he was ok and still with you. Have a wonderful Christmas, your husband will be right there with you. Blessings as always. Michelle

I said to my Angels - these feathers are not enough!

I was finding white feathers everywhere the week my son died. They were in places that couldn't be explained. However my grief being so heavy I found it hard to seek comfort. I remember sitting on my bed inconsolable and saying to my angels these feathers aren't enough, if u were really here they'd fall from the sky to give me a sign. I calmed down and suddenly felt exhausted I turned round to lay down, lifted my pillow at which spewed a million tiny white feathers all over my room. My pillow wasn't burst when I made my bed! I said "thank u" and had such a peaceful sleep. Xxx

Feather found after cleaning house!

Lately, I have had quite a few experiences with God, Angels and guides. Every one of these experiences have left me with a feeling of total awe and love. I was thinking about all of these happenings and asked my angels, particularly Michael, if they would please send me a white feather as validation of these occurrences. Also, if they wouldn't mind, to please do this within twenty-four hours. After this request, I went about my day. I decided to clean my house and went about the various chores. The last think I did was vacuum and mop the floors. When I finished I stood around admiring the results of my work. Everything looked great!! Happily I went upstairs to get started on the laundry. On the way back down the stairs I noticed something white on my black rug. I was a bit annoyed because 'dirt' was already being tracked onto my nice clean rug. I just vacuumed. I immediately to a tear in my eye and thanked my angels for bringing me this little white feather and what it meant for me. It didn't come the way I thought it would, nevertheless, here it is. Ask your angels for help and never forget they are there. They really are waiting to help us. Don't put limitations on them. They always figure out a way to get their message across.

Dear One, this is a perfect example of how our Angels give us a sign. No wonder you had a tear in your eye, how mischievous that they put it on your black rug. They knew you would definitely notice it there! Blessings Michelle

Feather in my kitchen

Hello! Everyone. I want to share something with you yesterday when I was coming out from Gym and I was on the road at that time I just felt that how life is beautiful, at that time one white feather fell in front of me then suddenly I realised that may be it was Angel near to me how beautiful experience it was isn't it? I didn't pick up that White feather but when I came to my home I found one small white and black feather in my kitchen and I kept it into my Angel feather box... ☺

Specially Thanx to Michelle for creating this page and I learned a lot about Angels from Michelle. . Thank you dear Michelle may God bless you ☺

Hello, I have a big smile for your happiness after finding your precious Angel signs. Blessings as always. Michelle

---

Grey Doves and Feathers

I have been finding feathers of Grey Doves what does this mean?

Doves are a sign of romantic love and grey is the sign of ambiguity. It there uncertainty in your romantic affairs?

Section 8

Angels and Children

Angels and Children

Children See Angels

Children are very in tune with Angels. Young children have not yet absorbed external programming about beliefs or perceptions. They have a purity and innocence which draws the Angelic realms very close. If a child speaks of an invisible friend or an Angel, believe them! Children will find great comfort from these beings of light and they will absorb their great teachings and wisdom.

If the qualities of children are left untarnished, then they have the potential to lead Earth to a place of peace in their lifetime. Encourage children to believe. Their belief in Angels gives them strength, wisdom, protection, hope and the greatest ability to give and receive love. Angels are a gift for everyone.

Encourage children to believe!

Children see Angels

Children feel Angels
Children know Angels

Children have hearts that are open
The Angels recognise hearts that are open

Angels enfold open hearts in their Divine Wings
Wings of love, protection and healing

Allow your children to see, feel and know their Angels

Angels and babies see and know their Angels. Speak to a child today and listen as they describe to you how an Angel looks. Listen to them as they describe to you how an Angel feels. More importantly, believe them!

Indigo, Rainbow and Crystal Children

Angels sing over Indigo, Crystal and Rainbow Children as they sleep. An **Indigo** child is a child that has a **pure vibrating aura**. This aura can be seen by clairvoyants as **Indigo in colour.**

The purpose of **Indigo children** is to help **raise** the vibration, **understanding and purity of humanity:**

- **Indigos** speak openly from an **open-heart**
- They **speak truthfully,** honestly, and with **integrity**
- To tell a lie, is not a possibility for an **Indigo**

Their **mission** is **straightforward, to lead** from the front, whilst speaking and **being in their truth. Indigos do not adhere to social norms,** doctrines, educational stances, politics, and religions. The only guiding light for an **Indigo** is **love** and **truth.** They demonstrate great **courage** in pursuing their goals.

Indigos are the children and adults of **revolutions.** They will use their **'sensitive'** natures to hone their skills to **serve for the greater good.** They will use s**peech, art, music, diplomacy, revolution even demonstration. But their underlying** driving passion is always that of **truth and love.**

Indigo children have an **affinity** with their **Universe,** their **environment, animals, peoples driving forces,** and **spirit.** They see and **profoundly understand** the spiritual realms. At birth they know **Angels, Unicorns and Nature Angels.** They know **spiritual truths**; they know the greater workings of things for the **greatest good of mankind.**

Indigos will **rebuke dogmatic educational regimes** which do not promote **heart felt love and integrity. They will reject those teachings that do not** resonate with **their deeply developed senses towards humanity. Indigos** know that we need to progress, in order to heal, to grow, and to ascend. **Indigo** children will **rebel against rules and regulations** which do not promote **self-expression and soul growth.**

Indigos love nature and **excel in natural surroundings,** in a concrete jungle, they will find it difficult and may suffer asthma or other psychosomatic ailments. It is as if they literally cannot breathe without the **life force of nature** to sustain and **nourish them.**

Allow indigos to choose their life. Their passions, their food, their, their hobbies, allow them to **find themselves.** They are **'innately'** already **in tune with their 'life-purpose'** and they will vigorously pursue it. They will do this regardless of governmental, financial, societal, educational or parental support.

The best ways to nurture your **Indigo child** is:

to just **love** them
to walk with them
when they follow their passions, allow them to voice their ideas
listen to the inner workings of their souls

These children are **gifted.** They are gifted with **extraordinary powers of right and wrong,** with no tolerance for falsity in any form.
Their **judgement** about people and situations is based on their **extrasensory** perceptions. These children are **psychic, clairvoyant, clairaudient, clairsentient.**

Crystal and Rainbow Children

Indigo children are **'powerhouses'** for Universal change and walking closely behind them now are the newer and gentler generations of **Crystal and Rainbow** children. The new generations of Crystal and Rainbow children **will take over** from the **Indigos,** once the major challenges have been transformed.

The **Crystal and Rainbow children** have all the qualities of the **Indigo,** but their **life-purpose** will be to **stabilise, nurture and support humanity** through its many changes.

Angels walk with **Indigos, Crystal and Rainbow** children. **These children are revered, protected and blessed!** **Angels** sing over these children as they sleep.

When a child is born

When a child is born a star ignites in the Universe
This star is the child's eternal guiding light

When your child grows taller this light leads them, protects them and guides them
Never will they feel lost, with the eternal light
Its bathing their soul with the protection of Angels

Mother Mary the Queen of Angels

Mother Mary works with the Angels. Mother Mary works with the **Angels of children** and the **parents of children.**

Call upon **Mother Mary** for help with all issues regarding **motherhood, children and parenting:**

- **Ask your Angels** to help you release and forgive any unhealthy patterns of parenting
- **Ask your Angels t**o help you release any learned or adopted patterns through your own childhood experiences and through the karmic family line
- **Ask your Angels** to open you up to **new parenting** possibilities
- **Release** the old and **'forgive'** yourself for anything you feel you may have done to contribute to these continuing patterns

Fertility

Your womb holds the blueprint for all things creative. Your womb holds the **'blueprint'** for all things creative and inspirational. Bathe your womb in the energy of **unconditional love** from the **Angels.** Be open to the possibilities of great expansion and expression in all creative, inspirational and nurturing endeavours.

Affirmations for Pregnancy and Creativity
- Mother Earth is now bringing me Universal creative energy
- I am ready to be a nurturing parent
- I graciously accept my creative powers
- I allow the creative forces within me to be released
- I allow my creative energies to work through me and bring me a healthy pregnancy and baby
- I deserve joy and I am thankful for the opportunity to nurture a new life
- I experience a profound connection to the miracle of life
- I now manifest my decision to have a baby
- I visualize having a baby now

Angels of Fertility

To ask for help if you want to start a family:
- Call upon **Archangel Michael** to cut the cords of fear. The **cords of fear** may be preventing you, **at some deeper level,** from being able to acknowledge that you are worthy to receive a baby
- Call in the **Angels of fertility**
- Ask them to bathe your womb and entire being in the **warmth and nurture of Mother Earth**
- Ask them to bathe every cell of your being in the **light of Angel love**
- Ask them to bath your womb so that it is healed and open to receive your **gift of a baby**

Release your requests to the **Angels**

Allow them to take it to the **heart of God**
*Thank your **Angels***
Babies are a Gift from God!

Are Cherubim, really child Angels?

Cherubim are one of the highest ranking in the Angelic Hierarchy. Their power is in their innocence, they have often been depicted by artists are children and babies to reflect their powerful innocence.

Cherubim are one of the nearest rank of Angels to God or Source. So they are the purest, finest and most innocent in the Angelic realms. They are the rank furthest away from human contact. They oversee the ranks of the Angels below. Through their innocence the Cherubim remind us of the freedom and purity of unconditional love.

Section 9
The Angelic Hierarchy

The Angelic Hierarchy

Angels belong to an Angelic hierarchy, where each level is assigned to the Angel, based on their service to humanity.

Sphere 1 - Seraphim, Cherubim, Thrones

These Angels serve as counsellors and are closest to God

Seraphim - First Rank, These are the closest to God and surround the throne singing praises.

Cherubim - Second Rank, are the Guardians of Light projecting from the Sun, the Moon and Stars. Their name stands for *one who prays* or *wisdom*.

Thrones – Third Rank, These are the Angels of the planets. Each planet has a Throne.

Sphere 2 Dominions, Virtues, Powers

These Angels serve as heavenly governors

Dominions - Fourth Rank. The Dominions advise the lower Angelic groups. They carry a golden staff in their right hand and a seal of God in their left.

Virtues - Fifth Rank. The Virtues transmit enormous amounts of light and are known as the 'shining' or 'bright ones'. They are thought to be the Angels of Miracles and Blessings.

Powers– Sixth Rank. The Powers protect us from evil beings and are believed to be the keepers of all the records held regarding our souls evolutionary journey – Akashic Records.

Sphere 3 – Principalities, Archangels, Angels, Guardian Angels

These Angels serve as heavenly messengers

Principalities – Seventh Rank. They oversee large groups and organisations. They guard nations, cities and leaders.

Archangels – Eighth Rank. Archangels watch over and direct groups of Angels, including aspects of Humanity. Most widely known Archangels include: Archangel Raphael, Archangel Michael, Archangel Gabriel.

Angels – Ninth Rank. Angels are most connected to the physical world and closest to humanity. There are many types of Angels with many different purposes. For example joy, healing, hope, love, peace.

Guardian Angels are the same category.

New Testament – Thrones, Dominions, Virtues, Powers, Principalities, Archangels, Angels

Old Testament – Seraphim, Cherubim

Which Angel to call for help

Physical Healing
Archangel Raphael - can be called to heal yourself and others.

Emotional Healing
Archangel Chamuel develops unconditional love and heals the heart and relationships.

Spiritual Healing
Archangel Zadkiel helps with gaining spiritual wisdom, understanding, detachment, letting go of painful emotions.

Education
Archangel Jophiel and the Angels of Illumination help with study and examinations.

Romance
Archangel Chamuel and the Angels of Love help with finding a soul mate and assist with relationship/emotional healing. They help the nurturing of love .

Protection
Archangel Michael, call upon him for strength and empowerment or for help with overcoming fears and negative feelings. Ask for help and protection to dispel harmful or negative energy. Call upon him for letting go of grief and sorrow.

Childbirth
Archangel Gabriel and Mother Mary help with all things to do with childbirth and midwives.

Transition and Bereavement
Archangel Azrael guides the departing soul on its transitional journey and can be called when someone is about to die. Invoke when praying after a loss or when remembering the birthday or date of transition.

Archangel Azrael's helping Angels: Metatron and Michael.

Archangels

What is an Archangel?

The word Archangel is pronounced (ark-an-gel). The term **Archangel** is derived from the Greek phrase *'the greatest messenger of God'*.

Arch means 'the first' or 'the greatest'
Angel means 'messenger of God'

An Archangel can therefore be described as an Angel ranked as the highest in the celestial hierarchy. The energy of an Archangel is powerful and strong. The vibration and tone is stronger than that of an Angel.

How to sense an Archangel

In the presence of an Archangel you may see flashes or orbs of coloured light. With practice and spiritual development you will be able to determine each Archangel as it becomes familiar by tone, pace or intensity. For example, the presence of Archangel Michael can produce a hot flash through your entire body. This happens as his powerful energy touches or merges with your own.

Do Angels get promoted to Archangels?

Angels do not get promoted to **Archangels**, but they are in constant training and their role or mission may change. **For example:** as we evolve so do our **Guardian Angels** evolve with us. **Guardian Angels** are beside us eternally

Archangel, why?

Archangel why did you stop at my house this night?

Archangel with your love of the light
Why did you stop by at my house this night?

Dear Child of God, no-one is forsaken. All will be embraced by the Angels regardless of creed plight or nation

But Archangel I am not worthy?
Dearest Child of God, you are on a journey to Gods heaven and, if you listen, this is known deep in your soul

But Archangel I don't hear see or know anything even when I try to believe?
Dear Beloved Child of God, your requests today now give us permission. Your knowing of us will now arrive. You will awaken tomorrow and in every direction there will be our signs.

Dear Beloved Child of God
This is your time!

Archangel Chamuel

Crystals – help us connect with the Archangels

Crystals have been in the earth for millions of years, absorbing the earth vibrations and its wisdom. They are therefore natural sources of energy which help to change the vibration of anything around them, including our environment and our body. They provide energy, healing and wisdom.

Crystals are natural energy absorbers, transformers (meaning they change energy), redirectors, healers and more. Many crystals are excellent for changing the vibrational frequency and overall patterns of our conscious awareness. Acting through the scientific principle of resonance, they influence the energy of our physical self. The energy becomes more like the energy of our non-physical Self. This makes it easier for us to communicate with intelligent beings, such as Angels, Guides, teachers who reside at higher planes of consciousness.

Crystals hold the energetic template and energies of the earth and transmit these energies even when they have been excavated. Crystals can help to realign the energy grids in your body and in doing so help to release stuck energies, emotions, patterns, toxins. This helps the body to self-heal and return to homeostasis (balance).

Archangel Michael - Blue or Gold Crystals
Tigers eye, Aquamarine, Turquoise, Lapis Lazuli

Archangel Raphael - Green or Deep Pink Crystals
Emerald, Aventurine, Chrysoprase

Archangel Chamuel - Pink or Orange Crystals
Rose Quartz, Kunzite

Archangel Gabriel - Indigo or White Crystals
Tanzanite, Blue Calcite, Iolite

Archangel Jophiel – Yellow Crystals
Golden Labradorite (sunstone), Citrine

Archangel Uriel – Gold/Purple Crystals
Angelite, Ametrine

Archangel Zadkiel – Violet crystals
Amethyst, Charoite

Archangel Michael

Archangel Michael is the Supreme Protector, who carries a sword in one hand and the scales of justice in the other. His blue cloak is often called upon for protection during meditation or spiritual development

Archangel Michael means 'He who is like God'. He is the great protector, physically and emotionally. He is the protector of humanity, the supreme overseer, who leads all Archangels in a 'legion of light'.

Archangel Michael is incorruptible. He carries a sword, as a symbol of his ability to cut away any negativity or fears from situations of your past, that no longer serve you.

Archangel Michael helps:
If you are being attacked, abused or feel unsafe
If you want to protect your home, possessions and environment
If you are under psychic attack or developing spiritually or psychically
If you want to cut the 'ties that bind' you to a relationship that has now finished

Archangel Michael helps us if we need strength or courage to change ourselves or our situation. He helps us to speak with truth, wisdom and integrity.

If we need Protection say '***Archangel Michael** help to protect me now from harm and give me courage and strength to face this situation. Allow the truth of this situation to be revealed so that I can be true to myself and others*'.

Crystals to use whilst working with **Archangel Michael:**

Tigers Eye - protects against negative influences
Aquamarine - enables you to speak your truth
Turquoise - protection
Lapis Lazuli - to voice your opinions

Archangel Michael says *'In my presence Dear Ones you may feel or see the colour of blue sapphire. You may feel the swish of my sword as I release you from unhealthy attachments. You may feel the strength of my protective shield all around you, protecting you from harmful energies.*

In my presence you will feel the strength to speak your truth, to act with integrity and to stand with power, even in the face of adversity or opposition. I stand beside you, to your right, at those times when you are in urgent need and have called upon me.

I will protect you as you sleep, as you walk, as you speak and as you develop your strength and confidence on your spiritual path.

Call upon me in any times of danger, in times of crisis, when you need more strength emotionally, physically and spiritually.

My blue aura will be placed around you like a cloak of protection. Pull the hood up and over your forehead to protect your spiritual eye, the chakra of clairvoyance. Know that with me by your side you have nothing to fear.

I am Archangel Michael, Warrior for Peace and Protection for all Mankind. This is my bond. My crystal is Lapis Lazuli, my tone is 'D' and my retreat can be found in the etheric of Banff, Canada.

To call me just say 'Archangel Michael, BE WITH ME NOW'!

Beacons of Light

Go forth, be a beacon of light,
Embrace the masses

Stand tall
Speak your **truth**
Speak with **integrity**

Hold your sword of truth firmly in your right hand
Be a **warrior for the light.** The **Heavens will rejoice** and the **Angels** will sing over you **Archangel Michael**

Angels that work in Archangel Michael's Team

Archangel Michael oversees a team of Angels on the inner planes. Archangel Michael oversees their tasks, their missions and their evolution and development.

Archangel Michael's team says to you, *'We are a team of communicators who protect through the spoken word and through our cloaks of protection. We stand with leaders who work for the light and protect people from those who do not. Our service is to be a blanket of protection from Heaven. No task is ever too large or too difficult as we serve with love in our hearts and peace in our souls. There can be no conflict where there is love and peace. Our mission is to restore the nectar of love and peace to all of humanity. We do this as our service to Archangel Michael and the God Source'.*

What is the God Source?

The God Source is the source of all that exists. It is the fountain of all knowledge, wisdom and unconditional love. There is no ego, just freedom. Everything is ethereal and sublime. Some people call this place Heaven. Heaven though, is not a place, it is a state of being. A position that is held by our hearts emotionally and spiritually. Heaven is a vibration.

God Source is above the void. The void is where all thoughts gather to create the external seeming reality. Fill the void with peaceful loving thoughts and this will be the reality.

The God source is unconditional love, which feeds down through the void to open hearts, awakened hearts. Awakened hearts feed the God Source. All other thoughts go to the void.

The progress of humanity is for the void to become filled with the energy of unconditional love. A void filled with unconditional love becomes the place called Seventh Heaven. Seventh Heaven is the place where God resides. God is the combined energy of all our thoughts, to create our reality.

The teachings of Archangel Michael

Forgiveness

Forgiveness is the healing balm for a broken heart
Forgiveness gives us back our wings
When we forgive, we are standing strong in our power, we are showing others higher ground. We are leaders and warriors for the light.

It is only through cutting from the hurts of our past, that we can truly heal, that we can rebalance, that we can strive for peace. Strive for peace now and in the future.

Peace is the strongest weapon we have in our artillery. Make peace, not war. Disarm others with your self-love, your open heart for all people, all faiths, all cultures, all Nations.

It is in peace that we truly stand tall. Be a beacon for peace and forgiveness today. Peace Be.
Archangel Michael

Unforgiveness - a stone in your heart

Unforgiveness is like a stone that sits in your Heart
It weighs you down and your spiritual journey is unable to fully start

As your soul opens a window, and becomes awake

There is now a brighter light intake

As you breathe in and out
The light dissolves the stubbornness of the dark and doubt

Once all the recesses have been reached,
a bright profound gem can now be seen

Where the stone used to stubbornly sit,
is now radiating a harmony of prisms and sounds

The crystal now swirling and glistening within, has been transformed into
a Diamond of Light so profound

Forgiveness and the release of Karmic Vows

Forgiveness is the release of karmic vows from your ancestry. Ask Archangel Michael:

To release the cords that bind you to family and personal patterns. Say *'Please release me now from the cords, patterns and energy imprints that confine me to a limited understanding of how to forgive'*.

Imagine his mighty *'Sword of Truth'*, integrity and fresh perspectives cutting through the cords that limit you to vicious cycles within yourself and in your relationships with others.

Thank your *'ancestral family'* for bestowing their gifts upon you. It is because of their teachings that you yourself have learnt compassion, faith, patience, tolerance and now forgiveness.

Forgiveness of ourselves and others is the *'key'* to the healing your heart. The heart of whole cultures and nations.

We are all mighty beings, who can stand hand in hand under and in the 'Light of God'. You can make a difference, change starts with just one step, one kind word, one wise person.

Blessings will be bestowed those who forgive
- Forgiveness does not mean that what you did to hurt me was acceptable
- Forgiveness means I will no longer hold on to those feelings that hurt me

Have compassion for yourself and others for the work ahead
Humanity must change and it is the enlightened ones who will be able to help the masses. Be in your light, be in your truth.

Stand tall say *'I am a child of God and the Angels surround me in their love, protection and wisdom. I am strong and I can make a change'*.
Blessings Dear Ones. **Archangel Michael**

What is Karma?

Karma is a Sanskrit word for balance. Karma is the evening out of actions from past lives or your reactions to your current life.

Sometimes a karmic event is set up in order for the other person to learn, whilst you gain a karmic credit for non-retaliation.

Karma is not a punishment. Karma is a strong spiritual tool to teach us how to take responsibility for our actions. In doing this we learn patience, focus, compassion.

Today is the day to release…

Today is the day to release. To release anything that no longer serves you. Call upon Archangel Michael. Ask him to cut the cords of attachment that bind you to:

Unhealthy people
Unhealthy patterns
Unhealthy mind-sets
Possessions, unhealthy circumstances

Walk away and feel the freedom as you realise your authentic self
As you find your peace, you act as a beacon of positive energy for others with your equilibrium and your spirit.

When everyone finds peace
We will have Heaven on Earth

Ask Archangel Raphael to heal you during your times of transition

Ask Archangel Zadkiel to transmute all lower energies with the violet flame, freeing you from stuckness and from stagnation.

With renewed clarity write down:

How your ideal life would look
How you ideal life would help you feel
How your ideal life would help others

Ask that the Angels bring you your ideal life, your heart's desires.

Everything is interconnected
Your growth feeds the growth of everyone, the entire Universe

Be the person who steps forward today and say *'I now relinquish all material, egoic and selfish needs and embrace the peace love and magnificence of freedom'*

In your place of freedom the Universe provides you with everything that your heart needs; unconditional love. Fly free. This is your moment!

Where there is unconditional love
There are Angels!

Now is the time to be Free!

Archangel Michael says to you *'Dear One, now is the time to be free!. Now is the time to release. Now is the time to be re-born.'*

With one mighty slash he brings down the sword and cuts the cords of:

- All the past
- All the anger
- All the sadness
- All the stuckness

You exhale deeply as the cords fall away. The entangled mesh of twine is lifted out of you. The 'Angels of Mercy and Love' carry the ball away to the heavens to be transmuted in the Light.

- Breathe deeply
- Feel all the restrictions gone
- Where there was stuckness you now feel the flow

Archangel Raphael says *'Dear One, now is your time to heal. I bath you in your entirety in my green healing light. Every memory, every cell, every part of your being is now healed. In all directions, in all time-zones, on all dimensions'*

Breathe in the green healing energy, relax. Know that everything you felt was holding you in stuckness, has now been transmuted, renewed, healed!

Step forward and say *'I am a Child of God, I now embrace my Divinity. I now walk forward in the full knowledge that the Angels are constantly at my side. Thank you Angels'*

Why is everything so difficult and never changes?

Personal relationships seem difficult because they present us with important changes to grow. Not every challenge is necessarily another lesson however.

Sometimes we can look at a repeating pattern, but this time we can respond differently or indifferently.

This is a sign of your spiritual progress. The challenges have helped you to assess your own integrity, honesty strength and spiritual viewpoint.

Now integrate all these skills and boldly walk forward. Thank your God for bringing you these challenges. These challenges have lead you to experience more personal and spiritual growth.

Challenges are blessings
Challenges are a gift

Embrace everything with an open heart. Walk boldly forward. The Angels rejoice as we step forward into our light.

It is in the stepping forward that we lead, teach and empower others.

No experience is ever wasted
No experience should ever be denied

All experiences earn us the right to walk along the spiritual path. Your Angels are always walking with you. Your Angels are always loving you unconditionally, protecting you and smiling at you with loving eyes.

Archangel Michael is a Warrior of Light and Divine Protection

His sword flashes sparkles of blue light, when he is in your presence. His sword cuts through the binding attachments that stunt your growth or freedom. Archangel Michael is a Warrior for peace and protection, his heart is gallant and pure. Call upon Archangel Michael when you feel afraid or when you want to move on from a situation. When you want to feel free of limiting beliefs.

Archangel Michael and Archangel Zadkiel working together create an almighty team. The 'violet flame' of Archangel Zadkiel helps to transmute the cords of attachment and create transformation in your life.

Together Archangel Michael and Archangel Zadkiel form an almighty team of cleansing and protection.

Archangel Michael leads you from the front. He leads you home to safety and keeps your spiritual mission protected and clear. He says *'Go forth dear ones, be guided by the light for Ascension. Lead with honour, hold your spiritual truth. Cut through all limiting beliefs with your honesty, integrity and passion'.* **Archangel Michael – The Warrior**

Dissolve your Pain – Become a Warrior of Light

Pain is an energy stored... deep inside
Behind your eyes it lurks and hides

Open up your sorrows to the beings above
Open up your pain to the Angels of love

They will bathe you in their supreme light
They will guide you through your darkest nights

Open up your heart to these beings of light
You will be bathed in their gold, purple and green healing light

You will emerge a Warrior ... strong
Filled with the Love of God

As a 'Warrior of Light' you can now boldly go
The Angels eternally your friend and not your foe

Do you have a Love of Fear?

Sometimes we only feel alive, accepted and validated whilst we are in the mode of fear! For example: anger, stress, victimhood, guilty, betrayed. But true strength comes from switching these patterns and realising that these modes of fear, are just illusions.

The only reality is love and to hold onto fear hinders spiritual progression. Always look at life from the perspective of love because this is the only reality.

- Ask Archangel Michael to bolster your faith in yourself so that you can feel strong enough to love.
- Ask him to cut away any negative patterns, any cords of attachment and cycles of fear that no longer serve you.

Now embrace your path to peace!

How to practice discernment

Discernment is the art of not just accepting a situation based on its face value. It is a powerful spiritual tool which can help us to protect ourselves from lower energies and to progress steadfastly along our path. We learn to observe potential pitfalls and diversions.

To show discernment is to listen to your intuitive voice about a situation. If your inner promptings are of danger or heed, then follow them. Our intuition is a powerful tool. It knows what is right for us and what is wrong for us.

Being spiritual is not about being sweet and nice
Being spiritual is about being honest, showing integrity
Being spiritual is about speaking from your heart with truth and conviction and showing discernment in your dealings with others.

Just because someone says *'trust me'*, does not necessarily mean that you must assume that they are trustworthy.

Discernment is one of the hardest lessons on the spiritual path. But to stand in your power means to stand firm in your judgement, even when things don't feel right for you.

Ask Archangel Michael to help you stand in your power. Ask him to help you stand tall, with strength and passion about the things that 'feel' right for you. Be a 'warrior' and protect your light.

Major Transformation – The Golden Age

Archangel Michael says *'Major transformation is upon us. Regimes will be disbanded, foreign legions will be disbanded. Good will prevail among all nations. Old routines and structures that no longer serve for the light, or the highest good, will be dissolved. There will be more uprisings, more revolutions, more disbanding of military regimes and dictatorships.*

We are now rapidly moving into a period of peace. The Golden Age. Angels are descending in their droves to be among us. Our role is to just be open to their love, their protection, and their teachings.

As the wings of the Angels join wing to wing, they will encircle the Universe. This will form a circle of winged protection. We will be lifted to higher levels of consciousness'.
Go Forth and Serve! - **Archangel Michael**

Protection for deeper spiritual work

Protection from lower energies is vital when working intensively with the spiritual realms and energies. The best form of protection is to only work with sources of known light like the Angels of God. There is no good or bad, but some spirits are not particularly wise and inadvertently, can cause confusion and chaos.

- Call in the light of 'Christ Consciousness' before undertaking any intensive spiritual work to protect your auric field.

- Ask Archangel Michael to enfold you from head to toe in his heavenly blue cloak of protection.

- Ask Archangel Zadkiel and his violet flame to purify you and release you from any patterns that no longer serve you in your spiritual work

Walk in nature often to heal your auric cloak
Sleep with fresh air around you
Thank the Angels!

As you walk the spiritual path you will be confronted

As you walk your spiritual path you will be confronted by fears. These fears are illusions, tests and initiations. At each point the goal is for you to undertake the next stage of your path with dignity, honesty and faith.

The more you walk with trust then the greater the love and peace that will be instilled into you on all energetic levels. The energies will reach you on all levels physical, etheric, astral, and emotional.

As you receive each influx of love and peace it starts to merge with all your cells and begins a process of healing. Each step of this healing creates an energetic and vibrational change in your being. Your consciousness begins to expand upwards and outwards. Above you is the fountain of all knowledge and its energetic resonance is stepped down in vibration to meet your current level of understanding

With each download of information
With each initiation completed
With each expansion of your consciousness

The chakras spin faster. Their energies become purer and their colours more subtle. The change in chakra energy and vibration affects your consciousness and is emitted out through your aura in waves. The new wave of energy then goes out far and beyond affecting the masses. You become a Beacon of Light!

At an energetic level you now attract people and situations that match your new vibrations and energy. The people and situations, even mind-sets from before, may now drop away or leave your scene. They are no longer an energetic match. Allow this process to occur, not with sadness but with the knowledge that this is a positive indication. It is a positive indication of how your spiritual consciousness is developing and growing.

Into your sphere, you will now attract new opportunities, people, mind-sets and consciousness. Concentrate your energies now on realigning, rebalancing and integrating all this new consciousness. Know that with each adjustment of light intake, there is also a purifying and releasing process.

Do not fight the process, go with the flow!
Rest if your body is realigning
Walk in nature and breath

- Ask the Angels to enfold you in their comforting, healing wings

- Ask the Angels to prepare you for the next step on your spiritual journey

- Thank the Angels for all the updates of new consciousness now and in the future
- Write down everything in your Angelic Journal

QUESTIONS ABOUT ARCHANGEL MICHAEL

Can Archangel Michael be in two different places at the same time?

Can Archangel Michael be in two different places? Can I call on him to protect someone in a different town from me as well?

That is a very good question. Angels and Archangels are omnipresent, this means that they can be with all of us at any time. If you want an Angel to protect someone in another place then this is wonderful. Archangel Michael is very good at protecting people. He will be very pleased that you asked him. Blessings Michelle

I need help for putting closure to a friendship

I need to ask my Angel for help repairing or putting closure to a friendship. I miss him and will always love him, if my Angel could just pass that along I would be happy.

Call upon Archangel Michael to help you cut the cords between you and your friend. These cords may be preventing you both from having closure.

Reply: I thought about what you said and searched for a little for what you said. I didn't follow through with the research. I went to bed and thought about Archangel Michael. When I woke I remembered a friend on

Facebook earlier that night had sent me an Angel to watch over me. He sent me Archangel Michael as well! Before I even knew what he did or what he could help with. I believe Archangel Michael has been trying to reach me as he knew I needed the help and didn't know how or where to ask for it.

Experiencing Archangel Michael

I love visiting churches and particularly when they are empty. I love the serene and quiet vibe. I can pray and meditate in total peace and harmony. A couple of days ago, I had quite a few different experiences in church. They were all spectacular, but this one in particular really touched my heart.

In this particular church I visit frequently, there's an altar for Archangel Michael. It is always my last stop on my way out. I leave a little prayer list and ask him to keep an eye on all the people on that list.

This time I stopped at Michael's altar and while I was praying I felt and saw a large man standing behind me. He was wearing a black suit and has Angel wings. The strange thing is I immediately realised this looked like John Travolta in 'Pulp Fiction', and I KNEW this was Archangel Michael. He smiled and just stood there like he was a CIA body guard. I smiled and said 'OK, let's go' He followed me out of the church and came with me.

As I was driving, it hit me that John Travolta HAD played Archangel Michael in a movie. I had totally forgotten about this. When I realised it he laughed and I got tears in my eyes.

You see, I never liked Archangels Michaels persona as an armour wearing Angel. It never struck me as right. I feel him as a strong warrior, but his love is so overwhelming I cannot relate to the armour. Archangel Michael figured out a way to let me see him in a way that would resonate best for ME.

He really wants me to share this with all of you. He wants everyone to know that we are individuals and as such Angels are capable of taking many shapes and forms in our lives. For me, he picked a form that I would find protective, but familiar. It would also let me know exactly who he is. He let me see the wings to make sure I felt and saw that he was an Angel.

Now they aren't there. I don't believe Angels have to have wings. It's their energy that speaks to me. He knows this. Michael says that for each person an Angel may come in a different form. Whatever that person finds the most acceptable.

Since this experience, I see Archangel Michael with me all the time. I always felt him there, but now I see him as well. I love that he did this for me and know that your Angels can do this for you as well. Thank you Archangel Michael. I love you.

I cut the cords to my friendship, but I want my friend back

Michelle, I asked St Michael to cut all my cords with one of my friends... I thought it was safe to keep friendship with that person... but when I again started talking to the person I wanted everything as it was before but still I was little confused and then I asked Archangel Michael, I said to him sorry and all and then I told him everything and I asked him for help and asked him and my Guardian Angel and Archangel Jophiel to show me correct way that whether I continue that or not... I have let that up to them now to decide the correct path and show me! Please tell me ... that they will show me!

Hello if you have love in your heart for your friend, and the relationship is a loving relationship, then no cords will become attached to you in the future. Cords only attach from people or possessions that are based on conditional love. There are no cords where there is unconditional love. Where there is true friendship the Angels walk with you. If this friendship ends then it is because one of you is now walking in a different vibration on your spiritual path. Whatever the outcome, know that everything is within the Divine Plan. The Angels love you unconditionally through all life changes. You cannot make a mistake, you can only learn. Blessings Michelle

Archangel Raphael

Archangel Raphael can help you to heal yourself and can help you to heal others. He carries a staff entwined with snakes in one hand, a bowl of healing balm in the other.

Call upon Archangel Raphael to assist you:

If you need to find doctor, surgeon, alternative therapist or need a medical diagnosis or surgery
If you need to have compassion, love and forgiveness or need help to heal others
If a loved one is sick or a pet is ill
If you are a researcher or medical scientist looking for a cure
If you are in pain, emotionally or physically
If you need help to heal your past
If a relationship needs to be healed and repaired

Say, *'Archangel Raphael be with me now to heal the wounds of my past, my body, my wounded spirit, to heal my pain, to make me whole again and to help me to heal others'*

Crystals can help you to connect with Archangel Raphael:

Aventurine - to open up your heart and teach you love and compassion
Emerald - to heal problems in the emotional heart, promoting harmony
Chrysoprase - activates and heals a broken heart, encouraging more love for yourself

Healing with Archangel Raphael

'Call upon me Dear Ones when you need to heal. Imagine me as a soothing balm of green healing light. This balm enters your being on many levels and cleanses you from all of the stuckness that is causing you dis-ease.

I can help you to release addictions
I can help you to eat healthily
I can help you to exercise
I can help you to think more positive

I and the nature elements of Sun, air and water work with you simultaneously to heal you cell by cell, memory by memory, emotion by emotion.

As the healing balm reaches every organ, every fluid, every space between every cell, you are renewed, refreshed, replenished.

Walk in the sunshine today. Feel the warmth of the Sun. Know that each moment that you call upon me a healing occurs.

Remember to eat healthily, plenty of fresh produce, from the local land, organic and pure. What you put into your body affects the vibrancy and health of every cell.

Fresh clean water helps your body with its natural healing system. Allowing it flow more easily. Allowing your natural healing mechanisms to happen effortlessly.

Your cells hold life, all life is sacred. The green healing balm will help you to nourish and protect this sacredness'.
Archangel Raphael

The Angels are in the air that you breath

The Angels are in the air that you breathe. The light of the sun, the sound of the wind and the beat of your heart. Your Angels are with you in each and every moment.
Draw your Angels close to your heart in each and every moment.
Angels draw closer when you are at peace. Still your mind and feel the Angels touching your heart today. A peaceful heart is a healing heart.

Where there is a healing heart
There are the Angels of healing

Affirmations for health and healing

- I am now healed on all levels in every part of my being. In all my cells, in all my fluids. I am now healed in all my organs.
- I am now healed in all time zones, on all dimensions, physically, emotionally, spiritually and psychologically. Thank you Angels.
- I am healthy and abundant. I release all anger, unforgiveness and fear, my cells are now revitalised with the light of love.

Archangel Raphael - Bathes all who call him

Archangel Raphael is the master healer and he bathes all who call upon him, in healing light. The healing light re-energises, renews and realigns, cells, body fluids and gases. It restores everything to perfect harmony and balance - Homeostasis

Archangel Raphael says

'Call upon me for an abundance of healing light, I will remove stuck and stagnant energies, and your cells will be glowing and refreshed. Release *fear, anger and unforgiveness, and feel your body returning to natural health and balance'.*

Healing on the inner planes

Healing on the inner planes is about Light and Sound

The sound of love
The light of love

When you follow a spiritual path dedicated to bringing in more light, then you are automatically healed. As you raise your vibration through this light intake you are eventually healed, renewed, restored and re-energised on a cellular level.

Ask the Universal healing team to take you to the inner dimensions during your sleep or meditations. Ask that you receive a one hundred percent increase in your light quotient.
Thank your Angels of Healing.

Can the Angels heal everyone?

Every soul has the seed of peace and goodness deep within. But many lifetimes of not being open to the light of the Angels has created layers, veils of illusions, karma and lessons which remain incomplete.

However, once the soul decides to open to the light, it starts to recognise that there is emptiness and void within. The layers can then be peeled back. The layers are peeled back by the light of the Angels. The journey begins.

As the journey begins the layers can be peeled back by addressing previous situations to balance the ego. Some paths are more complex than others. The Angels walk with us loving us unconditionally. Every step; a step of progress.

There is a seed of light within every soul, despite outward or seeming illusions. As Earth Angels we can help another to take the first step. We can be the love we would wish to see in another.

Ask an Angel to go to someone who has not yet recognised the availability of the Angels' unconditional love and light.

Ask that this person may *'for the highest good of all concerned'* have a profound angelic experience.

Is it possible that when I called for healing it wasn't granted?

A healing occurs where there is unconditional love. A healing is not a cure. A healing is the removal of a layer of stuck energy. Healing is holistic, it works on the energies of the body, mind and soul.

When you call upon the Angels of healing, you are calling upon their unconditional love. Layer by layer you will be healed. Layers can be formed by thought patterns, unhealthy patterns like addictions, karma, and ancestral karma.

In order for healing to manifest, then it is also a good idea to look at any pay off you may feel from being ill. At first this may feel like a strange suggestion. But an illness has an underlying emotional cause. Sometimes illness may allow us at some level, to just gain a little space. A little bit of peace and quiet, some personal private time where someone nurtures us. For a healing to occur, then you need to be open to the healing manifestation. You may need to adjust your eating habits, lower your stress levels or release some deeply held emotional trauma.

Ask Archangel Raphael to be with you. Ask him and his team to bathe you in his green healing light.

Ask Archangel Michael to cut through any cords of unhealthy attachments to people, mind-sets situations that no longer serve you.

Ask Archangel Zadkiel to transmute all lower energies and illusions releasing them and returning you back to your original state of Divinity which is full health.

Write everything in your Angelic Journal.

Healing is not a onetime event. It is an on-going process. It occurs layer by layer, emotion by emotion, cell by cell, moment by moment. As you feel things coming to the surface for release, repeat the exercise.

Each time you call your healing team your connection will become stronger and stronger. Look for healing signs and synchronicities. You may be handed a book on self-esteem, or healthy eating. You may receive promotional material for a positive thinking course. You may be guided to a natural healer, or specialist that understands your situation perfectly.

Thank the Angels and say healthy affirmations:

- I am totally healed in my entire being, my cells, my organs, my fluids, my thoughts
- I am totally healed on all time frames, on all dimensions and on all levels
- I am now vibrant and healthy
- I am totally healed
- I am renewed, re-energised and realigned
- I am healthy, vibrant and vital

When you call for healing a cure is possible
Where there is a cure, there is a miracle!

Where there are miracles!
There are Angels!

Angels today I ask for healing….

Angels today I ask for love and healing for…… (please insert the name of the person, situation, country or pet… that you need to send a healing request for) ….. for the highest good of all concerned. Thank you Angels.

Joy is the vibration of healing

It is in the joy of the moment, that a healing can manifest. A smile, a chuckle, a snort of laughter. All these joyful activities raise our vibrations.

When our vibration is raised, when it is fine and pure, the Angels can gather closer. When an Angel is close a healing must occur. Healing of the soul, healing of the mind, healing of the body, healing of the spirit.

Find joy today. See the fun. Feel the sun on your skin, smell the freshness in the air. Watch a small child and look at the world through the innocence of their eyes.

Lift your vibrations and embrace a healing today. When Angels gather close a healing will occur. Healing is the removal of a layer of stuck energy, emotional, physical, physiological or spiritual.

Archangel Raphael's' team of healers

Archangel Raphael is the energy of a supreme healer. His team work relentlessly with those people that call him to help them in all areas of health. He is an holistic healer working on mind, body and soul.

Forgiveness helps us to heal

A healing occurs when you release anger or hurt from your heart and replace it with forgiveness.

An Illness is unreleased anger, hurt or the feeling of betrayal. It is therefore unforgiveness of yourself and others. Once forgiveness occurs, then a healing occurs.

Where there is healing
There are Angels!

Pain Management

If you or a loved one is in pain then call upon **Archangel Raphael**.
Archangel Raphael is the master healer. Imagine the green healing light surrounding you or the person in need
Imagine the **green healing energy** entering **every cell** of your/their **being**.
Say, *'Archangel Raphael, may you and your team of Angelic helpers please be with, (insert name of the person in need of healing) now!... helping their body to feel well on all levels, in all time dimensions.
Thank you for your healing energy which is now helping (................) to feel at peace and full of energy and wellbeing'*

Breathe in the healing, blow out the pain. If you get repetitive feelings to help with the situation then follow them. Look for signs guiding you:

- You may feel like you want to place your hands over the affected area, whilst invoking **Archangel Raphael**

- You may feel that a warm bath or shower can help you to release the pain, imagine **Archangel Raphael's energy** is with you in the water as all the pain is washed away.

- You may feel like a walk in nature can help you, imagine the freshness of the outdoors, transmuting your pain

- Drink plenty of fresh filtered water to help your body flush away toxins.
- Call upon **Archangel Raphael** every day for help with healing and pain management.
- Remember to thank Archangel Raphael and his team!

Where there are **Angels**
There are **healing miracles!**

Depression

Depression is fear of the unknown and so a person holds on to an outdated notion. Depression is the suppression of anger and resentment and can be contained deep within, from many previous lifetimes.

Now is the time to release the past, now is the time to heal! Inside of you are energetic cords that are black and outdated. They bind you to unhealthy relationships and past situations. These energetic cords entangle within you, they unbalance you. They starve you of the positive life force from your Angels. The cords become enmeshed within you, like a ball of tangled twine.

Nothing can flow
Nothing can move forward
You are stuck!
Now is your time to FREE yourself.

Say, 'Angels please free me from the tangled cords that take my life force. Please cut me free from the thoughts, emotions, people, situations that no longer serve me. Please sever my attachments to situations, ideas, emotions that hold me in this stuckness'

Say, 'Angels please be with me now as I release, as I let go, as I renew, as I heal'

Now imagine the almighty Archangel Michael in his blue cloak of strength and protection, standing with you. He looks into your eyes lovingly. In his right hand he holds his almighty sword. With his left hand he reaches out and touches your shoulder.

Archangel Michael says to you *'Dear One, now is the time to be free! Now is your time to release. Now is your time to be reborn'*.

With one mighty slash he brings down the sword and cuts all the cords of the past, all the cords of anger, of sadness and stagnation. You exhale deeply as the cords are cut and fall away. The Angels of Love and Mercy carry the ball away to the heavens to be transmuted in the light. Breathe deeply. Feel all the restrictions gone. Where there was stuckness you now flow.

Archangel Raphael says *'Dear One, Now is your time to heal, I bathe you in your entirety in my green healing light. Every moment, every cell, every part of your being is now healed. You are healed on all levels in all time-zones and on all dimensions'*.

Breathe in the green healing energy, relax. Know that everything that you felt was holding you in stuckness, has now been transmuted, renewed and healed!

Step forward and say, *'I am a Child of God, I now embrace my divinity. I now walk forward in the full knowledge that the Angels are constantly at my side. Thank you Angels'*!

Write everything in your Angel Journal.

Addictions-at my lowest point I surrender!

Where there is a void, there is a spiritual path. Where there is a perceived need to enhance your body and mind with substances there is a spiritual path. Some people have a steeper more complex path, they can at times slip from their intended route.

Angels stand waiting. Waiting for the pleas of people who are trapped by the illusion of the void. When they hear *'Please stop this pain, this emptiness, this loneliness, this longing. Please help me. I surrender'!*

At this moment, the Angels hear us. They take us in their wings and they lift us to our feet. With tiny steps they walk protect, heal and nurture us. You are once again firmly on the spiritual path and you now know the signs. You follow the path called peace, love, healing and surrender.

It takes a strong spiritual soul to undertake the task of walking the spiritual path, in the stance of total surrender. In total surrender, we are in a place of supreme faith and trust. We have awareness that everything is interconnected. In walking the spiritual path we find everything we didn't previously know existed. In walking the spiritual path we find the things that we lost, when we took the wrong turn.

It is a very mature, wise soul who loses his direction but asks to be lead back. A wise soul with forgiveness in his heart and soul for himself and others.

Archangel Raphael and Abundance

Abundance is your Divine Gift

Abundance Dear Ones is your Divine gift from source. The Universe is plentiful and it lovingly wants you as a 'Child of God' to receive your heart's desires. Go forth with love in your heart and reach out your hand to Archangel Raphael now. Archangel Raphael is handing you a divine gift. It is an envelope and inside is written your heart's desires.

Accept the envelope and as you read out your heart's desires notice how you feel? Do you feel overjoyed, acknowledged, full of anticipation? Hold that feeling for a few moments, really feel it, breathe it, sense it and know it. In your hand is your heart's desires.

Now take your Angel Journal. Remembering all the feelings above write down each of your heart's desires one by one. Keep writing, make each desire as detailed as possible. Keep feeling what it would be like to receive it.

Angels hear your emotions. Emotions have a vibration. The emotions of love, joy, calm, peace and service to others create a fine pure vibration. The Angels can reach you more easily when your vibrations are pure and fine.

When you have finished writing all your heart's desires. Thank Archangel Raphael and his team. Know that he has completely understood and felt your heart's desires today. Where your requests are for the highest good of all concerned, then solutions and abundance will follow with Divine timing.

The Angels will provide, nurture and protect us

Money is a form of energy along with the energies of love, joy, happiness, and contentment. If you try to hold on to any energy you create an energy imbalance or block. You stop the natural flow. This block is called attachment.

Attachment is a fear based energy created by ego
Attachment does not come from a position of trust

The Universe will provide, nurture and protect us! Do not become attached to money. Allow money to flow in and out of your life in balance. See money as an energy that ebbs and flows. The ebbs and flows are created by our ability to detach from outcomes. They are created by our level of spiritual perspective. When you no longer hold on or grasp, the flow will begin again. When you release your fears and know that the Universe provides, you will have exactly what you need.

Visualise yourself as a 'Child of God'. Like any parent the Universe wants you to have everything that your heart desires. Open your mind and heart to the love of giving and receiving. Watch abundance in all forms flow to you freely and effortlessly.

Abundance Affirmations

- I now accept all the abundance that the Angels and the Universe want to bestow upon me
- I am now abundant in love, money, wisdom, joy, health, opportunities
- I give and receive in equal proportions to maintain a healthy flow
- I am a Child of God. The Universe and the Angels want me to have my heart's desires

What is the true meaning of wealth

The children in the world, who are suffering during this incarnation, are great souls. They have chosen as part of their life mission to serve humanity. They serve by showing the parallels and discrepancies between monetary wealth and spiritual wealth.

In obtaining financial wealth, possessions, luxurious goods, plentiful food, fresh healthy water and sanitation we do not necessarily have the experiences that help us to develop the soul. In having electronics which bolster our life, creating heat or cold, creating light and energy, we do not necessarily have the experiences that help us to develop the soul. The lessons of having plenty are to use things wisely and efficiently. Creating opportunities for others and dedicating our own intention towards *'how may I serve'*?

The wisdom within the soul of the poor is their joy, happiness and security from being able to appreciate the moment. From being able to be thankful for small mercies. For being able to show compassion and understanding to our fellow man and woman, our community. The wisdom of knowing that *'it is in the Being that we Become'!*

To be rich or poor, is not representative of how many possessions or honours you have. Or how much bank shares you hold. God and the Angels recognise wealth through the level of achievement in your soul. The achievement of learning and demonstrating qualities such as; love, compassion, selflessness, truth, joy, peace and community.

When a soul demonstrates love and peace in abundance then a person has significant wealth indeed. A person with an abundance of love and peace is also blessed with a wealth of spirit.

Angels rejoice and blessings will reach you tenfold
An abundance of love, creates and abundance of peace

Where there is Peace
There are Angels!

Abundance mantra: Love, Peace, Angels!

The Story of Poverty

One day a father of a very wealthy family took his son on a trip to the country with the firm purpose of showing his son how poor people live. They spent a couple of days and nights on the farm of what would be considered a very poor family. On their return from their trip he asked his son 'How was the trip'?
'It was great Dad'
'Did you see how people live'? the father asked.
'oh yeah', said the son
'So tell me, what did you learn from the trip'? asked the father.

The son said 'I saw that we have one dog and they had four. We have a pool that reaches to the middle of our garden and they have a creek that has no end. We have imported lanterns in our garden and they have the stars at night. Our patio reaches to the front yard and they have the whole horizon. We have a small piece of land to live on and they have fields that go beyond our sight. We have servants who serve us, but they serve others. We buy our food but they grow theirs. We have walls around our property to protect us, they have friends to protect them'.

The boy's father was speechless. Then his son added 'Thanks Dad for showing me how poor we are'!

This story is taken from a website 'A View on Buddhism' – Stories from the heart

Abundance

Open your mind and heart to the love of giving and receiving. Watch abundance in all forms flow to you freely and effortlessly.

Affirmations

- I have everything I need in my life
- My supply is limitless and I continually accept all gifts from the Universe
- I attract to me unlimited abundance

Which Angel do I ask for help with debt?

Who are the Angels I need to be asking for help for a lump sum money blessing to merchandize my poster artwork n eventually pay off my student loans and climb out of the abyss of debt I have allowed myself to create? HELP!!!

Abundance is a state of mind, an energy. When we have debt it is because our energy has become stuck with the thoughts of poverty consciousness. Work with Archangel Michael and Archangel Raphael. Ask Archangel Michael to cut the cords of attachment to poverty consciousness and then ask Archangel Raphael to fill you with the energy of Abundance Consciousness. Thank your Angels. Now go about your day being generous with your time and your love. Be abundant by acting abundant. It is in the Being that we Become!

Angels help you when you need financial assistance

One of my stories... I had gotten a bill from AT&T stating that I owed $88, from a go phone...I don't even have a go phone... So I tried all day to contact a rep to figure out this situation. FINALLY, this soothing voice answered my call. We both tried to figure out what was going on..to make a long story short, I did owe this amt from merging another phone line onto my line and it was a previous balance that somehow they showed it as a go phone,,,,,my heart sank because my hours had been cut for the last *two months and my finances were already so behind..I didn't know how I could make this extra payment...all of a sudden, after 25 min, Nick, said...mrs McClain... The only thing I know that I can do is just remove this from your acct. since no one informed you of this...I actually softly cried tears of joy and told him that he was my angel today...he was so sweet and then he told me that on his way to work that day, a woman's car was stalled in the middle of a busy intersection...cars were beeping at her, yet no one would help her. He proceeded to assist to moving her car off the road and she told him the same thing that I did...that he was her angel today!!! He was so happy to have helped us that day... I could hear it in his voice. He said i made his day and i told him the same..if i would have gotten in touch with a different operator that day, I'm not so sure that they could have done that for me...I really feel my angels had control of the whole situation to help me... I love my angels!!*

Animal Healing

Animals walk a spiritual path in the same way as humans. They all have souls with missions of their own to fulfil. At the end of their mission they return to the God-head, the Oneness, in the same way as humans.

Animal's souls are on a continuous path of evolution, as is Humanity. When we love and respect animals we allow them to fulfil their mission. Their mission it to bring peace, unity, understanding and unconditional love, to the masses. Their role is to lift the energy through their love on Earth.

We are all interconnected
The Love of one, affects the love of the whole!

How to give healing to your animals

Healing is unconditional love. Animals are very receptive to healing and just like humans can benefit from healing energy. Healing can benefit an animal emotionally, physically, psychologically and spiritually. If you have an animal then don't wait for an illness or stressful event to occur but instead practice being close to your pet and animal daily. Send them healing energy as often as possible.

How to heal your pet

Ask the Angels of Healing and Archangel Raphael to be with you to help your pet/animal.

- Sit quietly near your pet and ask it out loud if you can give it some healing
- Breathe steadily in and out, imagining your heart filling with pink light

- When your heart is full with pink light, rub your hands together briskly
- Tell the animal out loud that you are going to heal them now
- Put your hands onto the animal until your hands start to feel warm or tingly
- Now let the pink light, which is unconditional love to flow from your heart and down your arms. Imagine the pink light of unconditional love flowing out of your hands and into the animal
- Each time you breath in, the heart refills with the pink light
- Every time you breath out, the light travels down to your hands and into your pet
- Use your intuition to guide the movement and position of your hands
- Do this for as long as the animal is receptive. Normally 10 minutes is enough
- To finish the session, smooth the animal all over from head to toe
- Tell the animal out loud *'you will now start to feel better on all levels'*

Thank the Angels for their help and wash your hands under cool water to disconnect your energy now from the animal/pet. Go for a short walk in the open air.

A Dog walks

A dog walks as your companion, by your side
Every step you take, the animal faithfully follows
Every word, your dog faithfully hears
Every request your faithful dog fulfils with unconditional love
Your dog is an Angel, an Angel of Earth.
All animals are souls in a different costume.
Treat all animals with love and respect.

Where there is love for animals
There are Angels rejoicing!

Angel helped me with dying cat

I had been ill for nearly a year and for the first time in a year I ventured out with a friend on a short trip and we hit a cat. It was horrible! I hurried and pulled it out of the road and rant to houses nearby to call for help from either animal control, a vet or the police. None of them said they would come. The poor cats eyes were hanging out of its face, it was gurgling on blood and I was not able to make myself put the poor thing out of its suffering. But knew that I needed to. It's selfish to say I was suffering with this cat, as my pain was only emotional, but I was beside myself. Crying and shaking uncontrollably, when a young guy with a guitar over his shoulder seemed to come from nowhere and walked right up to me. He held me for a minute and told me to get in my vehicle and go home, that he would take care of it and make sure the cat suffered no longer. I was forever grateful for that. When I got home, my cat had given birth to kittens while I was gone. I know this was an Angel sent to help also…..!

Henry - the Heavenly Cat

I have a heavenly cat
It is a Divine fact
That he we was sent to watch over me…..

As I lay meditating, quiet and serene
Henry my cat, he approaches me
He lies upon my chest,
One paw upon my face, the other on a crystal, and together we rest

The energies move in and around, and begin to create a stirring
The Angels draw closer, and visit us both
My cat Henry, just lies there, purring

Henry, is a master I am sure of that
He senses when I am in need of love and healing
During our heavenly sessions he encourages me,

He looks into my eyes with meaning

As I am reading this poem aloud
He comes over to me, waiting for today's meditation to start!
Henry is a cat, an Earthly Angel
He creates profound love and healing within my heart

Archangel Gabriel

Archangel Gabriel's name means 'God is my strength'. Archangel Gabriel is often depicted carrying a golden trumpet, which he uses to awaken your inner angel and bring good news. Archangel Gabriel can give guidance and help with spiritual awakening.

Archangel Gabriel is sometimes known as the Angel of the moon. He uses feminine, intuitive energy to help with dream interpretation and visions. He uses the moon's magical energy to awaken humanity. He can guide you through life changing experiences, dissolving fear, by cleansing it in his white ray of purification.

Archangel Gabriel can assist you with purification if:
- Your body is full of toxins
- If your thoughts need to be free of impure or negative thinking
- If you have been sexually or physically assaulted
- If you are under psychic attack
- If your home, work or general environment feels negative
- If you feel that you have absorbed other people's problems

Archangel Gabriel can assist you with life changing situations like moving home, changing careers, undertaking new projects, starting a family, needing to understand your life purpose or mission.

Archangel Gabriel can help you with:
- Prophecy, inspiration and visionary matters.
- If your spiritual vision is blocked without any seeming reason
- If you wish to see Angels and their guidance
- If you need to better understand your inner world

Archangel Gabriel is one of only two Archangels mentioned in the Old Testament, the other one being Archangel Michael. Muslims say that Gabriel (Jibrail) awakened the prophet of God, Mohammed. Mohammed then dictated the Koran. The Koran is the sacred book of Islam.

Archangel Gabriel is known in Christianity for announcing the forthcoming birth of Jesus Christ, the child of Mary. Archangel Gabriel was present at the death of Jesus. He watched over the tomb and gave the news of the resurrection to the disciples.

Archangel Gabriel brought inspiration to Joan of Arc with her mission.

Prayer to Archangel Gabriel

Archangel Gabriel, in the name of love and light please guide me along my souls pathway by revealing to me my true purpose. Help me to understand my dreams and visions so that I am inspired and guided in the future during my life changes. Please help me to purify my body, mind and spirit of all toxic substances and thoughts. For the highest good of all concerned. It is done .....

The teachings of Archangel Gabriel

'I am the Angel of focus and clarity. I nurture you as you regain control of all aspects of your life. I bring comfort as you heal and release the past. I wrap my wings around you and I lift the blockages from your path ahead.

I listen attentively as you regain control of your direction in life and lovingly walk each step with you as you regain your confidence, self-esteem.

I appear to you as a being of white light. This white light helps to purify all aspects of your being. As you release stuck energies you feel invigorated, replenished, refreshed. Ready to start again on the road which leads you to your goals, your heart's desires.

I want you to achieve your heart's desires and I want you to be free of doubts. I can help you to heal your inner voice, your inner child. Take time to listen to this voice, it is the frightened aspect of yourself. Where there is fear, there can be no love.

Love heals everything unlike itself. When you call upon me I help you to lift this fear out of your heart and I help you to replace it with love. Inside your heart sits the inner child. When I bathe you in tender nurturing love, it reaches your inner child and a healing occurs.

Little by little, step by step your inner child releases all the wounds and fears.
Little by little, step by step, you heal your inner child and you become whole.

The wounds deep in your heart become healed. I bring you powerful nurturing like a mother or father. I bring you unconditional love. I lift you up. I help you to regain your inner strength. As you walk away from my healing you now walk with renewed confidence and grace. With your permission I will continue to walk with you'. Archangel Gabriel

Heal your Heart - Archangel Gabriel

'Dear Ones, Angels are always among us, you walk and talk with Angels. Each day when you go about your daily routine we are with you. We nurture you in our wings as we walk beside you. We speak through your heart.

When you need to hear, **we talk to you in the language of love.**
When your heart feels sad or broken, **we feel this too and we reach out softly to you**

Please embrace our compassion and love, this is our 'divine mission', to nurture, love and protect each and every soul.

We walk among you, sometimes we take on human form.
Sometimes we whisper in the wind, but mostly we 'dwell in the love of your heart'.

Nurture yourself, love yourself, and have compassion for yourself - the more love you have in your hearts Dear Ones, the easier it is for us Angels to be with you.

Today, start sitting in your own silence and listen to your 'inner talk', any fears or concerns block the flow of love. Dear Ones please hand over your anxieties and tensions in the form of words, thoughts or fear to 'us'.

We are here and ready to heal your hearts. Each chamber will be bathed in our unconditional love. Dear Ones reach out to us today'.
Archangel Gabriel

Heaven our point of purity

Keep on enjoying your journey
Every step is a step closer to purity
At the point of purity you are in Heaven

Heaven is not a place
Heaven is a state of mind, of peace
When you have peace you have Heaven on Earth!

Archangel Gabriel says 'You have a choice'

'Dear Ones, you have a choice. You have a choice how to feel, how to act, how to behave. No-one has the power to dictate to you how you should or shouldn't behave. The responsibility is entirely your own.

The world needs us to stand in our light and power of individuality. We need to influence others, not by anger, but through our integrity and honesty. The qualities of self-worth, begin with honesty, integrity and love.

The time is now approaching for all of us to play a part in shifting the vibration of the planet to a higher level. Angels are approaching Earth in their droves, they are here in many forms, they walk among us. Be sure to treat all who you encounter with the utmost love and respect. For the person you meet today may be an Angel in human form.

To have respect for others you need respect for yourself. If there are people or situations that undermine your self-worth then you must honour yourself, first and foremost.

Call upon Archangel Michael, ask him to cut away the cords that bind you to situations, people, possessions, even forms of thought that no longer serve you. It is only through releasing your 'attachments' can you move forward confidently and strongly.

Everything you need is freely provided by the Universe. Possessions only serve to bind you to attachments. Be free today of anything and anyone that may be stifling your true essence. Your true essence is light. This light is fuelled by love. This love is constantly replenished when you ask the Angels to be with you, to guide you, to teach and protect you.

Faith is the key. Have faith in the existence of an Angelic Realm. You will tap into an unlimited source of life, love and energy, guided by your higher self. Your higher self is an aspect of you that is enlightened and knows everything.

Make time to develop your relationships with the Angels every day. The word Angel has a high frequency and vibrates on the level of eternal peace and love.

We can all act like Angels on Earth. We just need to accept our inherent power to love ourselves and others. Spread your wings of love today and feel the vibrations of love emanating from you in all directions. Blessings Dear Ones' Archangel Gabriel

Angels Walk Among Us!

The planet has now started to move into a new era. The process began in 2012. All the new energies are beginning to touch Earth. The good work can now begin. We all have our part to play. The Angels walk among us! We can create Heaven on Earth. See everything in your life from the perspective of love.

Say to yourself 'What would my Angel say or do right now'?

Keep working with the master plan of the Universe, unconditional love. We can all learn to open our hearts and souls more and more. Little by little, day by day, moment by moment.

The rewards for love are greater than the rewards of fear.
The rewards of fear are illusions and are temporary in nature.

Love is the healing balm for our hearts. Each heart that heals creates a healing for the planet and Universe. Whenever you step out of the zone of love, stop!

Take a breather. Say to yourself 'What is the most loving reaction I could have in this moment'?

Always come back to the moment. The energy of the moment creates your future energy, your future experiences. To have peace in your future, then you have to experience love now!

- Walk in nature often, breath in. Still your mind.
- Ask the Angels to help you understand the synchronicities in life
- Ask the Angels for the life your heart desires
- Ask the Angels to help you, to teach you on life's' road through all its ebbs and flows
- Ask the Angels to heal you, nurture you and teach you about self-love

In loving yourself, you can love others.
Where there is love, there is peace
Where there is peace, there are Angels
Where there are Angels, there is Heaven on Earth

Heal a broken Heart

To heal a broken heart is to heal the Universe. For every crack in every heart is also a crack in the energy of the planet. Begin to repair old hurts, disappointments, abandonment and anger.

Bathe your heart in the healing white light of Archangel Gabriel. As the cracks mend, the energy from your heart cascades out in a glowing flow. The power is so immense and strong that it changes the vibration of everything around it, or in its path.

The energetic grid of the planet also begins to heal and repair. The new connections allow the energy of the planet to become finer and purer. With each heart that heals the planet is one step nearer to Ascension.

Dance with the Moonlight

Dance with the moonlight beams, upon us they pour
Sing with the rhythm of drums beating from far away shores

Lift up your heart to the Heavens above
Reach out with your hands and feel the Angel's beam of Love

Your Soul is your spiritual compass

Your soul is your blueprint for each lifetime. The amount of light it holds decides the pathway within each incarnation.

The soul has a vibration, a resonance. As more light enters the soul, the resonance becomes finer and finer. The Angels then find it easier to draw close to you.

Your soul is your Spiritual Compass. When it is healed in all directions you are fully awake.

Ask the Angels for help with healing your soul!

Archangel Zadkiel

Archangel Zadkiel means 'righteousness of God'. This Angel is often depicted as holding a dagger. He is the leader of the Angelic level called the Dominions. He is one of the seven great Archangels that stands before the throne of God. He teaches trust in **God**, and the benevolence of **God**, bringing you comfort in times of need.

Archangel Zadkiel works closely with the **violet flame,** a fast vibrating spiritual energy, that can be invoked to transform lower energies. The lower energies when transformed into positive emotions become the emotions of joy or emotional freedom.

Violet is the Ray with the shortest wavelength in the colour spectrum and as such has the highest vibration in the rainbow. It is the **Violet Ray** that is the transition between what human eyes can see and cannot see, becoming invisible.

The **Violet flame** is indicative of spiritual and divine alchemy and is therefore associated with transmuting energy from one dimension of physical reality, to another level, where things are yet to Manifest.

Call Archangel Zadkiel say *'please bathe me in your violet flame to help with any transformation of stuck energies and to help with my spiritual growth'*

Forgiveness

Archangel Zadkiel helps to transform through the healing effects of forgiveness and through the transmutation of stuck and negative energies. He helps with self-transformation and forgiveness through mercy and tolerance. **Forgiveness** helps to transmute stuck energies like selfishness, greed and anger which can build up and cause illnesses.
- if you want to transmute anger, unforgiveness, guilt......
- if you are unable to forgive yourself

- if you find it difficult to tolerate others
- if you find it difficult to be tactful

Transmutation of negative energies

to cleanse your body, mind and emotions
to purify all your chakras and your aura
to amplify healing or spiritual energies
to awaken the Divine seed within you , helping with your spiritual growth
to calm your mind before meditation, or to ease insomnia or nightmares

Anger an emotion of fear

Anger is an emotion generated by fear. There is normally a perception that something of value will be lost, someone's status, or reputation (as they see it). In order to maintain the external facade people create strength through the anger. Anger is used to deter you from the truth. But the truth is:

they fear that their perceived inadequacies may be exposed
they fear ridicule
they fear being shown to not be good enough

The person with anger is a mirror if we are on the receiving end of it. A mirror is always a correct barometer of how we are doing on our own spiritual path. We need to address our own underlying issues of inadequacy, our fear of exposure or ridicule. Our underlying fears of being betrayed, or abandoned.

When we recognise that these dark shadows are still lurking within ourselves, then we recognise that there is a need for more light. More light can heal and purify, allowing us to move into a higher vibration. Once the light of healing and purification have taken place then we can begin the appropriate work to release this pattern and the mirror will disappear from our view.

Ask the Angels of love and light to bathe the darkest recesses of your heart
Ask them to cleanse away any remnants of pain

Ask them to remove any bonding that no longer serve you

Breathe in the love and light of your Angels and allow stale, stagnant energies to be purified and cleansed. Allow any cords that have been binding you to be taken to God to be transmuted.

Any initial work or changes made to your energy patterns can stir up sudden volatility and unsettling situations, especially with people around you. This is a sign that you are changing. This external reaction is caused by the remnants of stuck energies now being healed and released.

As you change your frequency, it is like changing a radio station. At first everything seems different and not quite what you are used to, the switching between channels is fuzzy and distorted and you can't quite comprehend your new position clearly.

Then the new frequency arrives as you continue to adjust your internal controls. Once the new station/frequency kicks in, everything is clearer, more focused and smooth. You can now move forward confidently as you know your new frequency and vibration is beaming out loud and clear for others to enjoy.

The Anger is on another frequency, but you have now shifted to the frequency level of peace and joy. As the signal becomes ever stronger, then any occasional setbacks are quickly replaced, by you resuming your new frequency of peace and joy. Peace and joy are now your normal emotional level from moment to moment.

Anger is a major 'tool' of learning in our lives. Once it is addressed and replaced with confidence, assertiveness and honesty then a major spiritual initiation has been completed.

Archangel Zadkiel says

'I am the Archangel who clears energy blockages, stale emotions and auric miasms. I bathe you in my violet flame and burn through the dross which no longer serves your purpose.

Where cords have been cut, to release you of attachments, I burn the roots leaving no trace of the energetic imprint as that no longer serves you.

I can help to clear you from the energies of psychic attack and from the energies of emotional, physical and psychological abuse, in all time frames.

My light is a powerful purifier, raising your energetic vibration, as the debris that no longer serves you, is swept from your energetic fields and transmuted.

If you require a fresh start, if you require a vibration upgrade or if you just want to feel more free and uplifted within yourself, then I can help you. I can help you to achieve this and much more.

The transmutation power can be intense causing you to feel a hot flash or a raise in temperature. Call me frequently to clear your energy field of impurities, entities and miasms.

You will walk more freely once the debris and particles, that once clogged your energy field, have been transmuted. You will feel healthier, mentally clearer and physically like a burden or heavy layer has been lifted'.

Archangel Zadkiel
Master of transmutation

Archangel Chamuel

'Dear Ones, I am the Archangel of unconditional love and emotional healing. A healed heart is a loving heart. In the presence of a loving heart many blessings can approach you.

I, Archangel Chamuel come to you as feelings in your heart that feel loving nurturing and healing. I bathe you in a fine heavenly light. Its softness of tone and purity reaches all memories stored in your heart. If these energies do not resonate with the energy of love then a healing occurs. Any painful memory, emotion or heart break is healed in that moment.

Your heart swells with this cushioning of love, within its every cell. Where your heart feels blocked hurt or broken then I can assist you. In the presence of my energy you are healed emotionally as great waves of love can now reach you. As you now feel and emit your new heart felt love then more love is attracted to you.

Whenever there are heart felt interactions of love, know that I am with you. Archangel Chamuel is my name and I bathe you in the energy of unconditional love each and every day. Just call on me in your daily prayers'

Call upon Archangel Chamuel for the following:

to help you love and heal yourself
to help you feel love for others
if you feel lonely or heartbroken
to help you open your heart to finding new love

Life is a Journey

Life is a Journey together we travel
Sometimes, it appears that times are tough
Hand in hand, over hill and over land
Our hearts feel bruised and life seems rough

This is the time Dear Soul
The time that your Angel senses your need, the emotional pull
Do not feel that you are alone
Beside you your Angel walks tall

Always there by your side
Watching as the events of your life roll or collide
Ask your Angel to come ever close
Comfort she can provide

Soon you will see a clear road ahead
Your troubles and worries will now subside
Thank your Angels every day

Request with each step, remember to pray
With the embrace of your Angel close
Never from the path of love will you stray

Your Angel is your friend Supreme
With your Angel every moment is turning into a glorious day - Archangel Chamuel

Fiats to Archangel Chamuel

Please help my heart to heal by filling me with your unconditional light of love
Please help my heart to release any negative and stuck emotions from past relationships
Please help me to heal and dissolve any pain or negativity in my heart
Please help me to feel love for myself so that I can then love others

Teachings of Archangel Chamuel

Love is the Divine Essence

Love is the Divine Essence of your heart. This Divine Essence is visible to your Angel. Nurture yourself so that your self-love can grow.

When your heart is at peace, your vibration attracts many blessings, Angelic blessings. Love is the key to unlock your relationship with your Angel.

Say *'I am a child of God; I am a beacon of love and light. My Angel is by my side and loves me unconditionally'*

Never let anyone reside outside of your heart

Reach out with the light of your heart to everyone. Never discriminate. Let everyone be worthy of your heart felt love. Send the love. Never let anyone reside outside of your heart.

When you practice Love you find the answers

What is Light?
What is Dark?

What is Compassion?
What is Fear?

What is Forgiveness?
What is Hate?

The only question we really need to ask is 'what is love' And then we find the answers.

How do I find True Love?

The experiences you have of Love around you are a direct reflection of, how much love you hold for yourself and others in your heart.

True love is found within and then shown to you without
True love is not an external person or situation
True love is a state of being, a position of peace, contentment and joy

No external situation can affect the true love within your heart. Call upon Archangel Chamuel to help you fill your heart with the true essence of love.

Where there is love
There are Angels!

Conditional or unconditional love?

The path of love is plagued with self-doubt, jealousy and envy, guilt and inner turmoil. This is the path of *conditional love*

The path to *unconditional love:*
is awash with blessings
is awash with joy
is awash with happiness, hope and certainty

The path of love is one of the most difficult paths to master. With the support and guidance from the Angels then self-mastery of inner love, will be the starting point.

Angels guide us to self-mastery of inner love

Angels rejoice

where there is the vibration of love
when two hearts unite
when two nations ratify
when a flower reaches full bloom
when a child smiles
when the sun shines
when our hearts open

An Angel rejoices when we acknowledge the help that they can, and have already, bestowed upon us. As an Angel rejoices its light expands and this expansion is for the good of all. It is an all-encompassing light of love.

Manifestation of Love

The manifestation of love is one of your spiritual tests, lessons and initiations. Each encounter you perceive as love, is only a mirror of your own inner journey.

Where you see in another kindness, you are seeing the reflection of your own kindness. Each step towards love in the outer world, is one step towards love and healing in your inner world.

When you have peace, you have everything
When you have peace you have Angels abound

Love yourself today, giving yourself all the nurturing qualities that you yourself wish to receive from another. It is impossible to give without receiving. Give to others with an open healed heart and your love will be returned limitlessly.

Soul Mate

Our soul mate is the person who creates within us a trigger. A soul mate is either a person who pushes our buttons. Or is a person that understands our situation perfectly.

A soul mate can feel like our enemy as we vow to hate them. Or a soul mate can feel like a great person as we vow to love them.

A soul mate can stay by our side for a life time and will have been known to us many times before.
A soul mate can leave our side, but will have been known to us many life times before.

Anybody that triggers or pushes us to feel extremes of emotions is a great soul. This great soul mate, has chosen to work with you. This great soul mate has chosen to teach your heart about unconditional love.

Everything and everybody comes to us as a lesson or a gift. If you are lucky they are both!

Archangel Chamuel helps you find your life purpose

Your life purpose or mission will be the task or job that makes your heart sing and lift up. That job, hobby or task, where time just flies past and the enjoyment is in the doing, not in the receiving.

Your life purpose or mission is the soul contract you made before incarnation. You will be buffeted and nudged repeatedly by life until you find the exact groove. The groove where you wake up each day and say, ' *Yes, another lovely, wonderful day, doing the things that I enjoy the most in the world*'!

Do not follow someone else's plan for your life
Do not follow society's plan for your life
Follow your heart!

The finding of your life purpose or mission is a necessary part of your own spiritual evolution. It raises your vibration and this in turn serves your neighbours and the wider global community. Everything is interconnected.

Your inner joy, peace contentment and happiness will shine whilst undertaking your life purpose or mission. Your new energy will send out vibrations of joy peace contentment and happiness. Everyone will benefit.

Your heart sings when you find your life purpose or mission. Ask the Angels to help you. They will lead you to your correct life purpose and mission.

Find your life purpose, find your Peace

A person who sincerely wants to know their Angels will be guided each and every step of the way towards their life purpose. Your life purpose is the thing that your heart most enjoys doing and it helps you to serve others.

Your life purpose is that activity where you become absorbed with all your heart. The time flies, it never feels like any effort is required and it gives you the greatest sense of peace. This peace radiates out from every pore of your being. Others around you feel it, they sense it and they want it too.

What greater gift can any of us bestow upon another than the gift of peace? Be an example to others, a beacon. Find your life purpose. In doing your life's work you serve others. You also find your own inner peace and meaning. Write to your Angels today. Ask them to help you find your niche in life where you can be in your peace.

QUESTIONS ABOUT ARCHANGEL CHAMUEL

Can Angels help me to find love?

I know this is very selfish but I long for a permanent and loving relationship (marriage) with someone who would treat me with the love and respect that I would show them. A real companion whose needs I could put before my own. Can the Angels help with that?

Hello, yes the angels can help you with anything, they always hear your requests. Please look for the posts on how to ask Angels for help, how to write to them and how to sense their presence around you. Step by step they will show you signs and help you to gain confidence when looking for love, both in and around you.

Wanting to feel loved is in no way selfish, love is the greatest gift. So while you are waiting for this to come into your life, remember to love yourself a little more and nurture yourself.

Call to the Angels to help you with this. Concentrate on the qualities you are looking for in another and ask the Angels for help with finding that person. Then concentrate on developing those same qualities within yourself. Like attracts like.

In the eyes of the Angels is it wrong to be homosexual....

In the eyes of the Angels is it wrong to be homosexual or to have same sex relationships and marriages?

In reality there is no good or bad, there just Is! The Angels make no judgement. To make a judgement would be to have ego. Angels have no ego. They only know how to demonstrate the qualities of unconditional love. At a soul level everything is correct. Where there is a soul contract between two individuals then this is honoured, despite the gender of the flesh. The soul growth of each individual will be agreed before incarnation.

The Angels always rejoice in the presence of heart felt love regardless of the gender of the people involved. Regardless, of the gender, of the flesh. What is important is not the label of gender, but the quality of the union. The flesh can create many illusions, but the only reality is the vision and calling of the soul.

Where love is agreed between two souls then that will be honoured. This can extend to loving everyone you meet. We can feel heartfelt love for animals, for the Earth, for all people, all souls. It is the soul that must learn to recognise its calling to grow through the giving and receiving of love. The soul cannot flourish through labelling or constrictions of perceived societal rights or wrongs. Where there is heartfelt love, there are Angels.

In reality a vow to marriage is a societal role or label. The Angels only see the love between two hearts and as such this is the true reflection of bonding between two people.

Where a ceremony is held in celebration of soul love, Angels rejoice and oversee the proceedings. No judgement is made by the Angels regarding marriage. Only the intention of love between two souls is observed by the Angels. Where there is true heartfelt soul love, then the Angels can draw closer and bless the relationship.

Archangel Uriel

Archangel Uriel means 'the Light of God' and is one of the most powerful Archangels. He is the Archangel associated with peace, devotion, giving, receiving and service.

Archangel Uriel is a representation of Divine retribution and serves humanity. He can be called upon in times of crisis, like war and conflict. As an 'Angel of Peace' he can be called upon to bring about peaceful resolutions.

His colours are gold and ruby through to purple and he is often depicted carrying a staff or scroll. The staff is symbolic of your 'spinal column' and the alignment of all your chakras. The alignment of the chakras is necessary so that you are fully able to support yourself.

Archangel Uriel helps you to see clearly along your spiritual path. This helps you to recognise the needs of others and become less self-centred, promoting peace. He helps you to see the reason for being in this incarnation and helps you to ground your spiritual experience.

Archangel Uriel helps you to make your dreams a reality by helping you to identify the possibilities that you hold within yourself. He helps you to be innovative with new ideas and projects.

Archangel Uriel is associated with sudden change, thunder lightening and electricity

Call Archangel Uriel:
if you want to find inner peace, feeling unable to find stillness or calm
if you want to let go of inner turmoil and release fears and anxieties
if you want to find more stability in your life with your job, relationships or home
if you want to calm relationships that are in disagreement and volatile
if you want to release anger and irritation
if you wish for Peace to be bestowed upon the world, ending conflicts and suffering

if you want to give and receive in equal measure, especially if you have difficulty in receiving
if you want to release painful emotions
if you want a peaceful resolution to a problem
if you want to release your ego problems, and are boastful, impulsive and arrogant
if you feel insecure, mistrustful, apprehensive or shy
if you need inner strength and confidence

Fiats to Archangel Uriel

Archangel Uriel fill me with peace and tranquillity
Archangel Uriel release my fears!
Archangel Uriel bring peace to the world!
Archangel Uriel help me to serve others so that I can fulfil my life purpose!
Archangel Uriel illuminate my spiritual path!

Archangel Uriel says

'I am the Angel that give you a white peace dove to help you on your path of inner healing. When you see a white dove know that you are in the presence of my loving peaceful energy. My colour is ruby red through to deep purple and I help you to balance all inner conflict.

When you take flight with Archangel Uriel you see your life and its stories from a higher perspective. You see everything with a heart of love and you feel compassion for those who have yet to find their spiritual resources.

Let your peace dove fly free. As it reaches another destination it will share its gift of peace with many others. By allowing it to fly free you will also have allowed your heart to open even wider. For it is great wisdom that understands that nothing can be possessed, as we are all One. As one person heals, so we all heal. As one person finds peace, so we all find peace.

Allow your peace dove to fly! Your gift will be heaven. Heaven is not a place, heaven is a state of being'!

The teachings of Archangel Uriel

Wings of Angels Embrace

'Dear Ones, be in your peace. Know that there is love all around, that the wings of Angels embrace you and that they sing their heavenly prayers right into your heart.

The Angels cherish the love from your open heart and feed it as a reward. Your passion for Angels will be rewarded by your sense of peace, love and wisdom. These are all the gifts you will acquire when talking with the Angels.

Dear Ones, have faith, believe and trust in the heavenly vibrations of love that enter your very being when you call us. We always hear you and we always respond to you.

When you sleep soundly you have been protected by Angels. They are the gate keepers to eternal peace on Earth and beyond. Trust in your heart to lead you as it is through love that we teach. We lead you forwards on your life-long path home.

Blessings Dear Ones, may there be peace in your hearts' – Archangel Uriel

Peace Dove

A peace dove over and above does fly
Taking all remnants of unforgiveness up into the sky

A peace dove upon your shoulder does rest

You can now walk with peace
Spreading its energy out in all directions
North south east and west

Your works of peace are rewarded from upon high
With the peace Angels through a portal to heaven you will fly

The new frequency of Light

'Every person is now being bathed in a new frequency of light and at a cellular level there will be a profound change in how people view their positions in life.

People may feel emptiness as they search for more meaning. The Angels will embrace each and every one of us. From 2014 there will have been a mass undertaking of changes worldwide. People will be ready to work in co-operation, harmony and with more peace'. Archangel Uriel

Walk hand in hand

Together we all walk hand in hand
To higher and higher ground and we are merciful

Our reward is heaven sent, a badge of honour if we respect
The love of God is always within
It's eternally bathing everyone, every creed and nation.

The Universe is an eternal void

The Universe is an eternal void
An infinite void filled with energies

Each one of us supplies the void with part of its energy
Be sure to play your part
Fill the void with love, peace and joy

Fill the Universe with the qualities of the Angels
Angels are our friends Supreme

Archangel Jophiel

Archangel Jophiel means 'Beauty of God'. In the presence of Archangel Jophiel you will be helped with the awakening of your soul from its slumber. You will find wisdom, illumination, inspiration and joy.
Call Archangel Jophiel to assist you.

Energy Renewal

If you have lost your love of life
If you feel confused, and your thoughts are everywhere
If you feel like you have no inner light
If you have SAD - Seasonal Affective Disorder
If you feel the burden of worries
If you feel you have lost your sense of self - your personal power
If you want to boost your confidence and self esteem
If you need to heal your soul due to 'illness or shock'
If you need to release negative thought patterns or addictive behaviour traits
If you are full of self-doubt and fears

Inspiration

Call Archangel Jophiel if you need a creativity boost and have a creativity block
Call Archangel Jophiel if you need a fresh start in life
Call Archangel Jophiel if you are getting lost in fantasies and the whirl of thoughts
Call Archangel Jophiel if you need flashes of insight and need to solve problems
Call Archangel Jophiel if you have inner turmoil, tensions and conflicts

Call Archangel Jophiel for mental clarity when you need to take an examination and remember facts

Wisdom

Invoke Archangel Jophiel to connect with your higher self
Invoke Archangel Jophiel to seek inner peace and guidance
Invoke Archangel Jophiel if you need to integrate spiritual abilities
Invoke Archangel Jophiel if you need inner wisdom
Invoke Archangel Jophiel if you want to develop your intuition
Invoke Archangel Jophiel if you need to connect to the etheric realms

Understanding

Call Archangel Jophiel if you need to have a better understanding of yourself
Call Archangel Jophiel if you want to be able to understand others
Call Archangel Jophiel if you want some clarity with a difficult situation
Call Archangel Jophiel if you need to learn and absorb new information and skills
Call Archangel Jophiel if you suffer from paranoia and are self-absorbed
Call Archangel Jophiel if you want to understand your deeper self

Fiats to Archangel Jophiel

Archangel Jophiel fill my life with light, joy and laughter
Archangel Jophiel awaken my soul from its slumber
Archangel Jophiel inspire me with your wisdom
Archangel Jophiel strengthen my connection to my higher self
Archangel Jophiel change my whole being with your Light

Teachings of Archangel Jophiel

Who do I call for help with change?

As soon as you ask or think about change then it is guaranteed. Change is a natural part of everyone's progress spiritually, physically, emotionally and psychologically. If you need help with change then write to your Angels. Ask for everything that you need for yourself and others.

- *Describe in detail all the things you need to release in order to move forward*
- *Describe in detail all the things you need to receive in order to help you make these changes*
- *Describe how these changes will also help others*

Ask the Angels to help you, *for the highest good of all concerned.* Date your written requests, then put them away. Thank your Angels.

Your Angels are now working from the highest perspective to bring about these changes. Remember that Angels always see your highest potential. Nothing is impossible, in the Angelic realms, where you have made requests from your heart for the highest good.

Where there are Angels
There are miracles!

Trust that miracles can happen and they are already on their way

Life Changes

Life changes it is a fact
Every morning as we wake

We cannot use energy looking back

The next step we must fully take
The future plan of our happiness and fulfilment we must embrace

Take this moment
Take this present time
Feel it with hope, joy, love and your future will be Divine!

How can an Angel help with Self-Love?

An Angels love is pure and all encompassing. When you call upon your Angels they embrace you. They fill your heart and soul with their unconditional energy of love. A layer of the old will be peeled back and forever healed. You will feel it, as tears of joy are released. You will feel uplifted and as if your burdens have eased.

As you regularly feel these energies from your Angels, your heart starts to heal. You recognise the Angels healing energy, because it is the essence of your own soul.

Over time, including life-times, your soul has become enclosed in layers of false perceptions, fears and illusions. But as you peel back the layers you begin to once again recognise and feel the core of who you are. You are a soul, whose essence is divine unconditional love.

This moment is so powerful, your memory can no longer forget. The moment of awakening begins.

- *This is the moment where you remember how to feel love for yourself*
- *This is the moment where you remember how to feel love for others*

Gone are the layers of illusions, or fears. Your heart is free, expanded and all encompassing. People are drawn to your essence of love. Angels surround you.

This is a profound moment
A moment of enlightenment

There is no other route than the route of self-love. The more you heal, the more love you have to give. The more love you have to give, the more love you have to receive.
The love of your Angels is never-ending. Your heart will be continuously topped up.

How can the Angels help with breaking patterns of self-sabotage?

Self-sabotage is the illusion of fear. The illusion that you are alone. The illusion that on one hears you. Self-sabotage is the illusion of fear which causes you to feel that there is no way out. No way out but to punish yourself for your perceived failings.

But there are no failings, there are only experiences in each moment
- Don't label something or someone as good as bad
- Don't label experiences as good or bad
- Don't label yourself as good or bad

In reality there only 'is'. There is only 'this moment'. There is this moment, and then there will be another moment. When you feel the need to label yourself, your experiences or others then stop and listen! What can you hear, what can you feel, what do you sense. All this is in the moment of now! In the 'now' you can stop and you can decide *'Today is the first day of the rest of my life'!*

Then you can ask your Angels:
- Angels please surround me in your wings of love and healing
- Please release me from patterns that no longer serve me
- Please cut me from any cords that keep me attached to negative situations, negative people, negative mind-sets
- Please bathe me in your healing light on all levels and fill my mind with thoughts of joy

Thank your Angels. Now proceed to go about each day with a positive frame of mind and a joyous heart. Say *'Today is the first day of the rest of my life'!*

Say these affirmations:
- I am joyous
- I am abundantly blessed
- I love being me!
- All my experiences are teaching me
- Each experience is one step further along my path with my Angels
- My Angel is by my side and hand in hand we walk joyously
- We walk joyously along this lifetime's path, home

Write everything in your Angel journal and practice your affirmations, prayers and requests until you feel stronger and taller. Until you feel healed.

The Angels will hear you
The Angels will give you a sign

Be open to receiving and noticing their signs and synchronicities. They will place them, as well deserved blessings, along your path.

You have so much to focus on now, as your heart is filling moment by moment with light. The light of the Angels love.

The Awakening

As our energies become finer and purer our souls start to wake up. Our souls start to recognise that during their sleep a material world full of illusions has dominated. This has to date created our painful existence.

Our souls now realise there is another way, a different way. The constant pain of reaching, searching and longing are things that cannot ever fill the deep hole. The infinite hole deep within us. Not even ego driven pursuits like money, possessions, carnal love, drugs or alcohol can fill this deep void.

The only source that can quench this infinity of darkness, pain, grief and anger in our souls is the infinite source of love. The infinite source of love from your God and the Angels.

As our souls wake up we need to confide in someone, we need to trust in something. We need to hold onto something. Let Angels now draw closer to you. You now realise that this is the point of surrender. You no longer need to fight anymore. The Angel's wings wrap around you and all your sorrows are instantly lifted and you are left with the feelings of knowing that there is hope. You now know that everything has a much deeper meaning. You know experience colours, sound and smells as ethereal and heavenly.

But mostly you know there is hope. You know this because your soul feels able to love, not just others, but also yourself! It is at this point of realisation that a 'shaft of light' is felt going deep into the recesses of the darkness in your soul. As the light transmutes all your inner darkness, you are eternally transformed. You now see a clear path and you look carefully for the signs. You are now walking hand in hand with your Angels.

Enlightenment

Enlightenment is a state of realisation. A point where through your own eyes, and the feelings of your own heart, you realise that you do not stand or act alone.

You realise that a greater force is always protecting you and in a profound experience you feel totally safe and at one with everyone and everything around you. You cease to strive from a position of ego. You begin to walk through your life in the mode of 'how can I serve'?

Enlightenment is the point where your higher self joins with Source. Once this bridge is created, your whole perspective on life, material possessions, and the meaning of things changes. You now work for the greater good and no longer look from the perspective of personal gain.

The dichotomy is that in giving up everything in the state of surrender, you do in fact receive everything. You receive peace and an acknowledgement of the reason for your being. At this point of realisation profound joy, the love of Angels, and many blessings are bestowed upon you spiritually.

You are embraced by the generous, all loving, all encompassing 'Heart of the Oneness'. The Oneness is the heart of your God and is a place of supreme light, peace, love and joy.

To find enlightenment, dedicate your life to thinking, acting, loving with the qualities of your Angels. By becoming still and asking them for their assistance they will teach you, guide you and protect you eternally.

Enlightenment is a gift that is accessible to all. It starts with a state of surrender. Surrender is the position of letting go of your ego and having trust in the Universe to teach you. The Angels will always be with you rejoicing through this process.

QUESTIONS FOR ARCHANGEL JOPHIEL

I don't know if I am on the right spiritual path?

Hello can I ask a question please, how do I know if the spiritual path im on is the right one for me. I feel I should be doing more but im stuck, thank you x0x0x0x

You cannot be on the wrong spiritual path, as your path is unique for you. However, you may be stuck as you say due to lack of clarity and focus. This maybe because you fear making a mistake and feel overwhelmed with choice and directions. But there is only one choice, that is *'what makes me happy now'?* There is only one direction *'forward'*.

Go into your sacred space and relax into a deep meditation. During that meditation ask your Guardian Angel for everything to be made clearer to you. Explain your concerns, ask that your Angel show you clearly how you can serve? Thank your Angel. Take a breather.

Now come back to your journal and write down your perfect life as if it has already manifested.

How do you look and feel in your new life?
Who and what is surrounding you?
What are you doing that is serving others?
What is it that you are doing, in service, that feels so comfortable. It just flows?

Next time you meditate with your Guardian Angel imagine all these things.

Tell your Angel what this new life, is like, how it looks, how it feels, how you love your new role. Say *'Dear Angel, may this or something greater now manifest for the highest good of all concerned'.* Thank your Angels.

In your waking moments release this now and allow it to manifest with Divine timing. Set goals to walk one step at a time towards the manifestation of being in service.

Archangel Sandalphon

Archangel Sandalphon is one of the Archangels which doesn't end in 'el'. The ending 'el' means God in Hebrew. The name of Archangel Sandalphon means brother and his twin brother is Archangel Metatron. The twins are the esoteric expression of 'as above, so below'. These two twins are the only two Archangels who were previously mortal men:

Archangel Sandalphon was the prophet Elijah
Archangel Metatron was Enoch – a wise man

Archangel Sandalphon is known for promoting distance healing, planetary group healing and Earth healing. He unites the energies of Heaven and Earth, carrying prayers from humanity to God. Archangel Sandalphon is the Guardian of Earth and is personally responsible for the welfare of humanity.

The teachings of Archangel Sandalphon

The Awakening

Awakening is the realisation that there is something greater than self. It is the point where the heart opens and the soul responds. The soul sends a resonance of Universal love to the awakening heart, the light floods in. Light is consciousness. There is no turning back. As you start to awaken, there is a thirst for knowing.

Why am I here?
What is this life all about?
Why am I suffering?
What is God?
Why is nothing profound happening in my life?
Where is my Angel?

All these questions, feelings and agonies are your need for the light, your need to heal. This is the Awakening. There is no turning back you are now on your road to Heaven. Ask the Angels to walk with you and the road will start to unfold. It will become less of a struggle and more of a walk on a summer's day. You are no longer fighting with each step, you just go with the flow.

Every answer your heart requires in order for it to heal, will be provided. It will be provided by the soul in the form of synchronicity. These synchronicities provide learning points along your path. Before long, you will turn and look back. You will see how far you have come. From this point of acknowledgement you have peace. Every step of the road behind you, you were provided for. You now know deep in your heart, with absolute trust, that everything you need on the path in front of you will also be provided.

Walk tall, walk in your peace
Walk with your Angels - Archangel Sandalphon

Awakened Hearts beam out like Beacons of Light

An Angel sings at the break of each new dawn
each new dawn is our chance to awaken,
a chance to fill our hearts with the light
our chance to heal, to serve!

Serve with the Angels today.
Find your peace and shine your loving heart light like a beacon

Angels rejoice at the break of each new dawn
Angels rejoice at the sight of all newly awakened hearts
Awakened hearts beam out like beacons of light!

The Spiritual Journey begins

'Love extends from a spiritual heart and it travels. It travels to all recesses of the Universe. It shines out like a beacon, for everyone and everything to see.

The light from an 'awakened heart' is a very precious sight to behold. As it travels far and wide it touches all aspects, of all beings. A stirring begins. The souls that have been asleep, start to have a reaction:
They tremble and shake
They feel weak
Their anxiety rises
Their normal life seems no longer enjoyable or rewarding

There is a deep hunger for answers. Why, why, why?!
There is loss as things slip away
There is no longer the solid foundation below their feet!
They cry out. What is the meaning of life.....? Nothing resonates with me any longer.....?
Why do I feel different and displaced? What is happening to me?

The light is stirring in their soul. Their soul is starting to be become 'awake'. The spiritual journey begins'. - Archangel Sandalphon

What is the spiritual journey or path?

The spiritual path is the route your soul decides to take in order to grow, heal and expand, in each lifetime or dimension. Your soul will have decided before incarnation, the exact lessons, events and situations it will choose, in order to undertake these initiations of growth. Some souls decide not to grow or 'wake-up' in this incarnation and forfeit the choice to undertake the process called Ascension.

What is Ascension?

To Undertake Ascension your soul must have cleared all karma, and be able to demonstrate competence with all life lessons. This means being able to show integrity, compassion, love and wisdom.

Ascension is a process undertaken by some souls who have completed their life mission and are now ready to take the walk home. For those souls who do not choose a physical death at this stage of enlightenment, they then begin to experience 'Heaven on Earth'. Their souls shine out like beacons and this resonance has the capacity to guide, heal and teach others, through their example of how to walk the spiritual pathway.

- Ascension is the upgrading of energy in all beings on earth and within the Universe.

- Ascension entails deep purification, deep releasing of karmic and ancestral patterns.
- Ascension is the realisation of purity through deep cleansing and rejuvenation of the entire cellular and energetic synapses, structures, chemicals and cells of our body.

As each person purifies, releases and rejuvenates, then they begin a process of 'energetic elevation' called Ascension.

The process can be arduous and many souls will not complete the entire process this time around. For those who have dedicated their lives to this process then Ascension is guaranteed.

When many souls ascend to higher levels of energetic existence, then it is such, that the planet must also vibrate and exist, even finer and purer.

Ascension is not a possibility for everyone in this life-time, but the more steps you boldly take now then the less that will need to be done by others or yourself in other dimensions.

Everything is interconnected
Everyone's efforts help the whole

Archangel Sandalphon – Guardian of the Earth

QUESTIONS TO ARCHANGEL SANDALPHON

Why do bad things happen to good people?

There is no bad or good, these are labels created through the energy of fear. From the perspective of love all things happen for a precise reason, to teach our souls. As we learn, we heal. This is the primary reason for us being incarnated into the earthly realms. Nothing we undertake has not previously been agreed at a soul level.

In experiencing the many emotions of life, our soul becomes richer, wiser, more loving. It becomes more loving not only towards others but also towards ourselves.

When we learn to love unconditionally, then our lessons, tasks, and learning's will cease. The path of learning is lifelong. To develop unconditional love we need to be free of all ego. On the earth planes ego is necessary for our survival as it creates the passion for us to take action in our lives. It helps us to maintain a direction and focus.

As we walk along our path, unconditional love is our goal. We learn to encompass unconditional love more and more into our hearts. Our hearts then start to heal. When we have undertaken all our initiations successfully then our hearts are fully healed. We have now reached heaven. Heaven is not a place, but a state of being.

Every soul has a different path and may experience a different route to others. The wiser the soul the more difficult the path.

There is no good

There is no bad
There just is!

Ask your Angels to enfold you in their love. They will help you walk along your path with peace. Peace comes from knowing that no matter what the seeming external illusions, you are a child of God and as such you are loved, nurtured and protected by the love of the Angels.

Where there are Angels
There is Peace!

Heaven is not a place, but a state of Being

Sometimes it is hard to maintain the course?

The closer I get to the goal, the more distractions are placed in my way. Some days it is hard to maintain the course.

Distractions on our path are a sign of our progress. The distractions are the work of the ego and ego is fear. As we walk into new territory it is only understandable that we may allow fear to step in. However, remember this, 'you are a Warrior of Light' and the distractions and their intensity are a measure of how far you have come.

- Spend some time just sitting in your peace
- Ask the Angels of love to draw closer and ask them to help you feel their peace on all levels
- Breathe it right in, right in to every cell

Know that any distractions are a sign of progress and whenever you feel a little lost, come back to the moment again. Keep asking the Angels of peace and love to walk with you.

Archangel Metatron

Archangel Metatron's name translates into 'great throne' or 'to measure'. He is the Angel of Ascension and can also be referred to as: Angel of the Presence, King of the Angels, Chancellor of Heaven, Chief of all ministering Angels, Angel of the Covenant.

Archangel Metatron is the twin of Archangel Sandalphon. He resides in the seventh Heaven and Archangel Sandalphon resides in the core of the Earth. The two create the bridge between Heaven and Earth. Archangel Metatron was once a human being like Archangel Sandalphon. Archangel Metatron was previously Enoch who vanished from Earth. He didn't die an ordinary death but was taken by God directly to Heaven (Genesis 5.24)

Archangel Metatron has a throne with the other Angels ministering beside him. He wears a crown with the Holy Letters (YHVH – Yahweh). This stands for God itself. He was elevated by God to the highest divine status possible, where he was bathed in clothes of light and given supremely human qualities.

Archangel Metatron is able to speak many languages including the language of animals. He is able to assign great royalties, gifts and greatness upon earthly people. Archangel Metatron, like God, has 72 names, one of which is Jofiel, or Jophiel – Beauty of God.

When you call upon Archangel Metatron you can shed any illusion of separateness and release karmic bonds. You can surrender to the divine power and become at one with the Divine. Archangel Metatron is also known as the liberating Angel. He releases us from earthly duty at the time of death.

In the presence of Archangel Metatron a brilliant white light is seen. It has overwhelming radiance. His presence can help us to bring about dramatic spiritual transformation in our lives. This can help us with our enlightenment, light-body activation, and our Ascension into higher levels of understanding and perspective. Archangel Metatron is often referred to as the Angel of Ascension.

Vast Light – Christ Consciousness

Where there is light beaming from a heart
There is the greatest awareness of unconditional love
Where there is unconditional love
There is the vast potential for a miracle, for a cure, for hope

Let the vast light of Archangel Metatron beam directly into your soul and fill your entire being. His frequency of truth and God Consciousness is the highest and most almighty, apart from Source itself.

Archangel Metatron has been bestowed with the qualities of teaching Christ Consciousness. Christ Consciousness is the highest and purest form of healing energy currently available to us. Behold the light of Christ and you behold the heart of 'your God'. Archangel Metatron advises us 'to be still and patient before the Lord'. He prophesises that the 'meek and mild' will inherit the Earth and he reminds us, that all human deeds, will eventually have to be reconciled and justified.

Archangel Metatron is mightier than Archangel Michael. Both have been described as heavenly scribes.

Akashic records

The Akashic records are kept by the highest order of the Angelic realms. Archangel Metatron oversees the Akashic records. Angels, who work as scribes keep a record of each soul's progress. Including things to be learnt, initiations successfully undertaken, possibilities for future realms of existence. No judgement is made at this level about your progress. Only your God, the Source can decide. The Angels are purely the note keepers.

Archangel Metatron says

'The eternal awakening of the soul is called Ascension. Those who journey to Ascension are eternally healed and eternally blessed with the presence of Heaven.

Heaven is not a place
Heaven is a state of BEING!

I was once a mortal man, Enoch. I stood before God in a state of Surrender. I was chosen as part of my Divine Service to be the Angel of the Presence. The Angel of the Presence is the job of the Angel who is chosen to sit beside God. To the left of God. My mission is to teach all within the Angelic realms and beyond, about the eternal mysteries of life. About evolution, about the raising of consciousness for all of eternity.

I am a Guardian for the Light. The Light of the Cosmos and beyond. To access my energy then all lower energies of ego must be mastered over many lifetimes, through initiations that are presented with ever increasing stature. These initiations help the soul to grow eternally strong.

I work with Archangel Michael who resides on the right hand side of God. Together we oversee an almighty team who are helping to raise the consciousness of humanity for the continued expansion of our Universe and Cosmology.

I am the only Angel able to look directly into the Light of God. God is the culmination of wise and loving thoughts. Pure, but difficult to describe in the earthly realms. The purity is what gives God its immeasurable strength and ability. This purity can transform and transmute anything and everything. God is the energy of love. Love is pure, so vibrant and vital. God is love. Love heals anything unlike itself.

In my presence you will find enlightenment. You will understand the meaning of interconnectedness. You will totally and profoundly understand the meaning of 'we are all One'.

Once you have reached the spiritual perspective of knowing and feeling my energy, you will have activated your soul star and Ascension chakras. Your chakras will glow pearlescent white, and shimmering. Your chakra column will merge into one column of light called the Antakarhana or rainbow bridge.

You are now able to access the wisdom of God directly through me. Your Ascension journey will now have begun. Ascension is the bringing down of light or consciousness into every aspect of your being. Ascension is the journey home.

Molecules are the basis of all life, all living matter. The essence of love has the power to propel this life forward so that there is evolution, peace and joy.

Bathe in the Metatron cube of life. Its Divine love will combine with the essence within your heart. It reaches you through the window in your awakening soul. You will be bathed in such a vibrant heavenly harmonic of sound and light, that you will become eternally awake and enlightened.

The metatron cube is the route to the healing of Metatronia. Imagine yourself within the metatronian energy cube and you will be eternally upgraded in your energy and healing on all levels. Working with Metatronian energy is a slow and steady process. The spiritual foundations must have first been deeply developed and all prior passing of initiations must also be in place.

Archangel Sandalphon helps you to ground all your initiations securely. Working with Archangel Sandalphon and Archangel Metatron simultaneously will help your energies to be evenly developed preventing them from becoming displaced'.

Teachings of Archangel Metatron

What does everything and everyone is interconnected mean?

Everything in and around the Universe is energy. One particle of energy cannot move, without affecting the whole. In the same way, we are also beings of energy, every emotion, every thought and every word. They all affect the energy around us. It affects the whole.

Sounds have energetic resonance and vibration
Thoughts have energetic resonance and vibration
Feelings have energetic resonance and vibration

Every thought, feeling or sound we vibrate is heard by the Universe. The Universe accommodates this by realigning itself. In realigning itself this affects the whole. When our energy is of a hostile, negative or critical vibration then is affects the whole in a negative way!

When our energy is calm, peaceful, loving and compassionate then this affects the whole in a positive way! Think, feel, speak and breath with the energy of love and see the world find peace. Everything and everyone is interconnected!

Ask the angels to envelop you in their wings of love to help you. Find your own inner peace. Be a beacon of light, peace and love for the entire Universe today!

When one person finds peace, we all find peace

Walk hand in hand

Together we all walk hand in hand
To higher and higher ground, and we are merciful.

Our reward is Heaven sent, a badge of honour, if we request
The Love of God is always within
Its eternally bathing everyone, every Creed, and Nation.

What is Enlightenment?

Enlightenment is the knowing within every cell of our being that something greater than ourselves exists, penetrating every aspect of our lives, every aspect of the Universe.

It is the realisation and deep knowing that everything is interconnected and that we are all protected by the infinite love of the Universe, the Source, the Creator and God.

Enlightenment is the profound realisation within all your senses that everything and everyone is interconnected and that all is One!

With my heart I give you my Love

With my mind, I absorb your wisdom
With my hands I reach out to touch your Angel Wings
With my heart I give you my Love
With my entire body and eternal Soul ,I AM

Ascension the raising of awareness and a healing for the whole of humanity

Ascension is the progressing of our eternal planet. The raising of awareness for all of humanity. The process to date has been long and arduous, but now energies flooding all of us from the Universe are stabilising thousands and thousands of years of Divine Evolution.

Many symptoms in your body and mind will arise, sometimes causing a temporary mania, but this will quickly pass. It's a sign that you are realigning physically, emotionally, psychologically and spiritually.

Ascension is a holistic process for the whole of humanity. As we all join together the process will become more subtle and sublime.

A new humanity will be bestowed upon all mankind.

- More community
- Less corporate status
- More emphasis on love thy neighbour

A stripping back to the basic values within all Humanity, to be loved and to love. Today, we must hold out our hand to our fellow companion on this evolutionary path.

As we walk together
The Angels walk with us

Those of us who are sensitive's are the way-showers. From our open healed hearts:
- We all walk out, at the front
- We can put up the signposts for those fellow humans who have become lost in the cycle of re-incarnation. Who are lost in the mist of uncertainty and indecision
- We now create a clear example by who we are, by how we allow ourselves to be motivated by our passion for love
- Our passion for truth

- Our ability to detach from illusions
- Our ability to see the bigger perspective for the whole of humanity

As an Earth Angel and light worker our path has been complex, arduous and not without pain or loss. Now we look out and we see how everything is in a perfect landscape. The landscape of the Divine, Divine Perfection.

We are now approaching the Oneness. Our journey to lead others is nearing completion. There will be much rejoicing and fanfare by the Angels. We are creating Heaven on Earth.

I give my life in service...

Thank you Angels for your love, protection, wisdom and grace. My life is now service to the achievement of these qualities for myself and others. May this or something greater now manifest for the greatest good of all concerned.

The Golden Age

Archangel Metatron, was the overseer of Atlantis. Atlantis was a city that was only accessible and visible to those people who resided in the seventh dimension of existence. Atlantis will not return, but a new 'Golden Light' is starting to emerge. We are moving into a new Golden Age.

Before the Golden Age can be fully established all financial, political and cultural regimes will need to be realigned. The time is now coming. Many Angels are among us helping with this work. All those who work for the 'light', should step forward now, and take their places in service. Shine your light into all that you think. Shine your light into all that you do. Shine your light into all that you say.

The Golden Age is divinely decreed. It will occur either with simplicity and smoothness or with trials and difficulties. The souls on Earth have the choice. Those who choose to 'be awake' will help the others.

A miracle is upon us....

A miracle is upon us
The birth of a Golden Age
A time of supreme manifestation of peace, guidance, and love from the Angels

As you gaze upon the wings of your Angel
You gaze upon the future of the Universe
Pure, omnipresent and joyful

Miracles are upon us
Where there are miracles
There are Angels

Your Golden Aura

Pave the way ahead with Gold
Not the Gold of money, but the Gold of Enlightenment

Your Golden Aura
Becomes the colour for wisdom
Becomes your colour for grace
Becomes your colour for unconditional love, peace, joy

Gold the colour of Angels
Breathe in the colour of Gold
Breathe in the colour Angels

The Angels of Change are Among Us!

There are currently intense changes occuring for the whole of society. Reforms abound economically, politically, financially, and in the arenas of health.

The changes are purification for all souls who have been operating from pure ego and not from love. The new energies now upon us have been readying for over 26,000 years and now is the right time. There are enough souls among us who act as 'beacons of light'. We have been tested, nudged, pummelled, expanded and energetically realigned, it has been a gruelling process.

Now the alignments, the grids of light for the entire planet are nearing completion. This will not be an end to the world, just an ending in the way we currently respond and act within it.

We now have a new beginning. Now is the time to have hope and to realise the gifts are not necessarily financial. The gift of 'being at one with others' will now be the driver within all awakened and awakening souls.

Embrace the newness, for the future paths are unwritten. Those working for the light can now step forward and energetically create the pathways for all other souls.

This task in the past has been strenuous, exhausting, but now the energies will lift you. You will glide into your positions, your motivation only to embrace everything with love, compassion and Oneness!

Those people who do not serve the light will either pass or choose to become 'awake'. So strong are the Universal energies now, that no soul cannot hear.
Embrace your divinity
We are all of the oneness
We are all beacons of light
We are all children of God
Blessed are those souls who work, walk and embrace the light.

We are not teachers, we are awakeners

Archangel Azrael

'Know that your loved ones are still beside you on the inner planes. Their love for you is their eternal bond and promise. Help your departed ones to be free and happy on their new path. They will never leave your side. In releasing your departed ones you can heal your own soul. Your unconditional love is recognised by God and Source. Many new blessings will be bestowed upon you.

Life is a circle, it is never ending. Sometimes it changes direction and route. But we are all walking towards the light, at whatever stage of soul progression we currently hold. Walk your path with pride. Hold your head up high. Say' I am a child of God'. Feel it, sense it, see it. You know it is true, when your heart, which is a barometer, allows you to feel your God and the Angels as they surround you in their peace. The Angels of peace walk with you' – Archangel Azrael

The light of Illumination

Archangel Azrael is the master of transition. He is the master of overseeing departing souls. He is gentle and wise. His only desire is to escort a transitioning soul to the light. He also bathes those grieving in the Light of Illumination.

The Light of Illumination is the understanding that death is not an ending. Death is a beginning. Archangel Azrael teaches other Angels how to work specifically with the newly arrived souls. Archangel Azrael teaches other Angels how to comfort those left behind, through the many stages of grieving. These Angels stay until there is the Light of Illumination.

In that moment both the departed soul and the grieving soul, suddenly know and recognise, that they are eternally bonded. They recognise that not even different dimensions of existence or vibration can ever separate or prevent that. The Light of Illumination is the turning point! The Light of Illumination helps us to understand that the bonds of love are eternal.

Archangel Azrael is the keeper of souls on the inner planes. He bathes, heals and nourishes departed loved ones. He sings over them, he comforts them. Once the soul is renewed and refreshed, it then returns to the Universal planes in order to undertake the rest of its journey. Each step, a step closer to Ascension. At the point of Ascension the entire soul merges with the light. The soul is now able to serve on a much greater scale for the whole of humanity.

Archangel Azrael is also the overseer of those souls who are still on the earthly planes and are grieving. He takes them in his wings of love and softly and gently strokes away any loss and pain.

Your tears are Angel medicine
Your tears heal your soul

Departed Ones have freedom!

'Release your thoughts of pain or sadness, over departed loved ones. Now bathed in the 'heavenly light', they sing, they laugh, they have joy. They are free!

Gone are the struggles and initiations, symbolic within the human flesh. They are now:

Free to merge
Free to love
Healed and free!

Ask the Angels to help you release your on-going grief or pain. They will surround you and enfold you in their love. They will lift you to a different space.

You too will become more free. You will experience their eternal love. You will know that your continuing journey, no matter what stage, is a blessing in your life. You will know that it is overseen lovingly from above.

Let your emotions fly free, soar up high, feel the light, the sun, the wind. This is your true soul strength, freedom' – Archangel Azrael

Archangel Azrael – works with the departing soul

Archangel Azrael is the Archangel who works with the departing soul. He is also the Archangel who bathes and supports people who are grieving for their loss.

Death is not a sad occasion. Death from the higher perspective is a joyful reunion of a soul with the light. Death is a time of introspection and preparation for the next stage of the souls' journey.

Grieving for a lost 'loved one' is a natural human emotion. In time it is however, in the interest of the departed one, that they be fully released with love. The departed soul can then go about their daily mission on the inner planes.

Our loved ones do not leave us. Our loved ones continue to serve on another dimension and are always showering us with love and compassion from the inner planes. Occasionally, a departed loved one will re-train and return to our side as a 'spiritual guide'.

Your loved ones say *'release us lovingly to the light, so that we can freely walk, retrain and complete the next stage of our ascension. You are always in our hearts, we see, feel and hear you. When it is possible we send an Angel to give you a sign. We try to send you frequent signs of our love and peace from the place of our new existence, Heaven. Heaven is a state of mind, not a physical place'.*

Archangel Azrael – Keeper of the Light says *'Dear Ones, release your loved ones to the light and never fear that they are eternally lost. In fact they are eternally blessed. When you release them it helps them to reach their place of Divine blessings, with more serenity and with more peace.*

They know you are now able to go on, in the knowledge, that they are eternally by your side'

Ask your Angels to comfort you

- Ask the Angels to comfort you during your different stages of grieving.
- Ask your Angels to lift any despair or longing or sadness from your heart and to bathe you in their healing light.

Over time, this process will open up a new window for you, a new perspective. On the horizon you will look out and you will see a new dawn:

- a bud on a flower
- a spring born animal
- you will look out and you will know that the cycle of life is eternal
- you will know that the bonds of love are eternal
- your will know that the love of your departed one, is in fact, in everything and everyone you see

Call upon Archangel Azrael to comfort you during your stages of grieving. Write everything in your Angelic Journal. Grief is a process, a personal process. One step, one emotion, one memory at a time. Angels comfort you.

Teachings of Archangel Azrael

The Angels who oversee Death

Angels of death and transformation come to us when it is time for the soul to move to another dimension. The silver cord of life is temporarily removed and you travel to a resting place, Bardo. In Bardo you are bathed, cleansed, healed and in some cases retrained for your next incarnation. The records of your life are analysed by the Lords of Karma. Your soul makes a new contract to negate any outstanding karma or initiations in future incarnations. Other souls agree to re-incarnate with you in order to teach you and help you with your soul's lessons.

Once all karma is complete
Once all the life lessons are complete
Once all soul contracts are complete

Then we can return at a soul level back to the light, to serve humanity on a much larger scale. The Angels of Death escort us to the appropriate place once the soul leaves the human body. The Angels of Karma oversee the Angels of Death.

The Angels of Death are very loving, nurturing and protective of the souls they are transporting. They bathe the soul in harmonic sounds and the healing balm of light.

Is there life after death?

Death is an illusion. So life continues, but in a different dimension, form or time perspective to what we currently call life. It is as if we have stepped from one room in our house to another, or from one level in our house to another. The soul continues long after the human body has been removed, or ceased to exist.

Death is an illusion

Death is an illusion. It is just a doorway through which we step up to the next stage of our journey. We are still connected on all levels to the ones who love us, this continues for all time.

Death is an awakening. It is the window through which we can see clearly. We can make amends for our previous life and rejoice at all the Blessings we have now earned. These Blessings help us on our way to Heaven.

Heaven is a state of total peace and contentment
Heaven is a place of calm, stillness and complete silence
It is a place of unconditional love. There is now no human form, to create restrictions, there is only pure energy. Death is a blessing, a release. Death is a new beginning.

When your soul has completed all its contracts with others and fulfilled its mission, then it will be your turn to step through the doorway to Heaven the place of supreme unconditional love.

As one life passes by

As one life passes by
An Angel sighs, 'You have missed me. I waited for you to call to me, to ask, to reach out your hand to me. I waited, it is my job you see? Now my service to God will be re-evaluated, as I wait for my next mission'.
Your Angel

- Call out today
- Hold out your hand today

- Ask your Angels today
- Help an Angels progression in Heaven

Ascension

A Soul that passes with no karma, having completed their life purpose and with a high level of consciousness (light) will Ascend.

These Souls have the choice to serve as an Ascended Master either on the inner planes, or they can choose to return to Earth to serve. They will return free of Karma with a role of teaching others. This process is called Ascension. When we Ascend we are spiritually pure light.

Every Soul has a destined amount of time on each level of its journey based on how many spiritual initiations are undertaken and how quickly. The wisdom of the Soul however is not necessarily measurable in terms of years in incarnation. The Soul's wisdom is measured in terms of spiritual consciousness or Light.

People who have walked as Ascended Masters include:
Jesus
Buddha
Krishna
Sai Baba
Mother Mary

A miracle at the end of the current road

At the end of this current road
A miracle begins to unfold

All these tests that previously had gone before
Have now lead me to this magnificent opening, the Golden Door.

As I boldly, through it step

I look back at the people I have left in my wake

But there is no sadness, not a drop
For in front of me, is my everything. Angels of God

Their wings are magnificent and opaque
They embrace me and my loved ones who are feeling such heartbreak

The wings of the Angel are magnificent indeed
They create a swooping cape of Love around me

The wings of the Angel are magnificent indeed
I know they will protect me and my loved ones for all Eternity

QUESTIONS ABOUT TRANSITION

When is it time for a soul to pass over?

How do we know the signs that a soul is passing over. Why do some people fight it?

A soul passes from one dimension to the next when it has completed everything it had contracted to do. The soul is eternal.

Some people appear to fight the process of 'passing' because there is something they have yet to complete in terms of soul growth. Or they may fear what lies ahead of them on the next stage of their journey.

It is important for a soul to realise that, it in only the physical body that dies, that the soul is eternal. To keep the vision of love and peace within and around us at the time of dying, makes the transition easier for the soul.

No soul is punished at the time of their physical death, instead their soul is taken to the serene place of 'Bardo', where the Angels sing and bathe you in their healing love.

At the appropriate time the soul will then decide the next stage of its journey. Depending on its current level of soul knowledge the next journey will be carefully planned to strengthen those skills and areas of knowledge that still need to be gained.

What is the oneness? What is Bardo?

The Oneness is the place where all energies of peace and unconditional love merge. This peace and unconditional love create a resting place for all souls.

So does your journey end here?

No, this is the place of rest, between each incarnation, in between each lifetime. The Oneness is the experience of Bardo. Bardo is a state of suspension. A state of Bliss. A state of regeneration and renewal.

At the end of each Soul journey or lifetime the soul is returned to the state of Bardo. The Karmic Board, Guides and Angels then decide with the soul the purpose of the next mission.

The Soul then incarnates at exactly the right moment with the blueprint of this lifetime's mission or life purpose deep within. At exactly the right moment, the soul remembers and can decide to become awake. This life time's purpose begins to then unfold.

Do people who commit suicide go to Heaven?

If a person commits suicide, do they go to Heaven, I was told that they did cause God knew what was on their mind, had a nephew that did, he left no clue.?

If a person commits suicide, then they had not yet successfully completed everything that their soul was contracted to do, on this level of their journey. As their soul passes they will be prepared to begin their journey again in another form. This is so they can complete that aspect of their soul growth. Heaven is not a place, but a state of being. So once the soul recognises that the only reality is love then they are in Heaven.

In your Nephews next incarnation he may choose a role where he himself teaches others how to achieve this state of peace. His soul will recognise that any early departure was not the way and he will help others to finish their soul contracts.

On passing, your nephew did not undergo any pain or stress. In fact, it was the opposite. He realised that what he already had was the opportunity for Heaven on Earth.

He is peaceful, calm and wise now because of his experience. This man is happy and will at some point reincarnate to share his new perspective and happiness by helping others. Your nephew is a beautiful sensitive soul, he loves you and is always with you. Blessings, Michelle

Why do some mothers lose their baby's.....?

Mothers who lose their children are **great souls, Mahatmas.** They have chosen at their deepest soul level, to learn one of the hardest spiritual tests, the test of **unconditional love.**
In the loss of a child, our heart learns and recognises, that the only reality is love, **unconditional love.**

Every moment is Divine
Every breath is a Gift

These **initiations** serve the mother ...... and the **Angels see** her. They see her tremendous **Strength.** They see her tremendous **Heart.** They see her tremendous **Love.**

In that moment, there is the possibility for all **karma to be dissolved** and a clear route home will be possible. The **mothers of departed children** are **great souls.** The **Angels, love cherish and protect** these souls. There is no greater spiritual sacrifice, than the **letting go of your child. Call upon the Angels and Mother Mary, the Queen of Angels, for comfort and support**

What is the Spiritual reason for Stillbirth or Miscarriages?

For some **souls** the process of **incarnation** is traumatic. As the **soul** leaves their **previous existence** and comes through the birthing process, they are thrust into the three dimensional **reality of Earth**. If the **soul** is sensitive then leaving another plane of existence, even though it is their choice, can be extremely traumatic. In leaving behind their previous level of happiness they also leave behind a fragment of their **soul**.

Some **souls** cannot make the transition and are **born still** or they decide they cannot make the journey to this dimension **this time around**, choosing instead to **miscarry**. The **parents** of these **souls** will have chosen the lesson of losing a child as part of their own **soul growth**. They will have decided upon this before their own **incarnation** or before the pregnancy.

The **soul** of this baby was chosen to match the exact **soul growth** for everyone concerned
The parents who choose these situations are **wise souls,** on **steep spiritual paths.** It is important that these **wise souls** understand the meaning of this process so that they do not hold blame in their heart or guilt. It is important, despite your loss, that you show **love and compassion towards yourself** as you would to another. **The Angels see your wisdom and strength.** In the face of adversity you become a **beacon for others.** Your **strength love and forgiveness of yourself**, will **inspire others** to lead more **tolerant, loving and forgiving** lives. Your rewards are in **Heaven.**

Heaven is not a place
Heaven is state of being

Find your **peace**
Find your **Heaven - The Angels Walk with you!**

Do babies become Angels if they die?

My baby daughter died long time ago, did she became in my angel????? Some people said me that!!!!

Hello, how lovely to see you today. I am sorry to hear that you lost your precious baby daughter. In answer to your question, Angels have never had a human incarnation and as such your daughter will not have become an Angel.

However, when loved ones leave us on this plane of existence, they do not go far, it is just that we cannot see them with normal eyes. The bonds of love between us and our loved ones are eternal and as such your daughter will have always been by your side and may even be guiding you from spirit.

If you speak to the Angels about your daughter then you may receive a sign from them to let you know that she is indeed very happy and is with you. The bonds of love are eternal. Blessings dear one, lovely question. Michelle

Abortion, Pastor said I cannot be forgiven?

I don't think that angels believe in me anymore i have been told by a pastor that you cannot be Forgiven for an abortion I have strayed from god since. Please tell me it's not true.

God does not make a judgement. God is all loving and gave us **free-will**, so that we could experience things to help with our **soul** growth. In developing our **soul** we find great **gifts. We find love, compassion and tolerance.**

Some lessons on the path to developing our **soul** seem intense, mystifying, even surreal. We think, *'this is not my life'*! Never did we imagine that such a difficult situation could occur for us. We had made such different plans.

But at a **soul** level, *'this is our life'*! We have never been given any lesson by the **soul** that God didn't agree that we could handle. **This has been a tremendously hard path for you,** so far you have been walking uphill and it has been so steep. But today is *'the first day of the rest of your life'!*

The Pastor is himself having to walk a difficult path. The Pastor has chosen to walk the path of Dogma. Each scenario presented to him, that is outside of this rigid framework of teaching, will make him act judgemental and he will need to repel it. **But the lesson for the Pastor** is to **face his** own inner **Soul** and to ask himself, *'in what way do I make **judgement** about myself and others. In what way do I criticise myself and others. In what way have I been impatient and intolerant of myself and others. In what way am I not listening to my own heart and integrity'*?

Everything in our outer life is a mirror of the progress of our inner soul. The forgiveness that I see most outstanding in this situation, is forgiveness for the Pastor. Until such a time, as the Pastor can forgive his own shortcomings and face his own soul lessons, then he will continue to project his own fears onto others.

He will continue to not own his own lessons, instead projecting them onto others and labelling them as a direct interpretation of God. God is all loving, all encompassing. God does not make a judgement.

You do not need God's forgiveness as you Dear Child are made in Gods essence. *'Today is the first day of the rest of your life'*! As a Child of God, your only task today, is to have compassion for yourself. Compassion for yourself, not because you have done something wrong, but compassion for yourself, for ever thinking that you had done something wrong. *'There are no mistakes, only learning's'*.

Dear Child, *'This is the first day of your new life'*! Ask your Angels to shine a bright light now, onto your new path, and they will walk with you. All the emotions of this event, have given you great experience, and if you combine this experience with the tremendous love you hold in your spiritual Heart, then you Dear Child will walk as a Beacon of Light. You Dear Child can show others the way. *'Today is the first day of the rest of your life'!*. Angels Walk with you .

I am so angry with our Angels, they have taken my dad suddenly.........

Im so angry with our angels right now, they have taken my dad suddenly, not dealing well with this at all :(

I am very sorry to hear about the sudden loss of your father. I totally understand that you feel angry and don't feel able to cope, who would? The Angels though did not decide to take your father, he would of decided this at a soul level before incarnation. The only involvement of the Angels would be in helping him during his transition to the next level. For yourself, remember that Angels are our greatest friends and they will want to help you through the different stages of your grief. Take a moment Dear One and ask your Angels to help you with your shock over this sudden event. They will hear you and your Guardian Angel will wrap her wings around you. When it feels overwhelming talk to your Angels about everything, and write to them about it in your Angel Journal. The Angels will send you some sign of their presence, you may feel them around you. Let me know how you get along. Blessings dear one...... everything will be ok...... Michelle

Guardian Angel comforts me

Hello☺ Im new to this page I believe I have a few guardian angels looking over me at the moment .. lost a loved one and been finding feathers and feeling a presence.

Hello, I am sorry to hear that you recently lost a loved one. Please work with Archangel Azrael at this time, he will help you with all aspects of your grieving process. It is absolutely correct that your Guardian Angel will have drawn closer to you at this time, and the feather is your sign that the Angels are there to comfort you. All you have to do Dear One, is ask your Angels for what help you need. They are indeed waiting to reach out to you even more. Write everything in your Angelic Journal, this will help your connection and will also help you to heal your heart. Blessings to you as always precious lady. Michelle

Wonderful moment

Hi I must tell you about my experience with AA Azrael. At 12.15am on 11/11/11 as I lay in bed unable to sleep I felt my third eye being worked on. I was told that i was going to experience something that day. My friend called me and asked me to visit her mum who was in a care home and was dying. About 20 mins after I arrived I saw AA Azrael standing at the bottom of the bed. I noticed that he had huge wings and commented to my friend about them. He informed me that this was so that he could put his wings round and comfort the spirit on their journey over to the other side. He told me that he was always with my friends mum. This was a great comfort to her. When I got into my car to drive home I realised that this was why my third eye was being worked on in bed that night, and this was what they had informed me I was going to experience. Thank you AA Azrael for that wonderful moment

An Angel is at the Bridge to Heaven

A river flows by my side and across the bridge I can see a light
This light is the light of unconditional love, it is the light of my Angel

As I walk towards the bridge, the path changes, twisting and turning. The scenery changes, the weather changes. But as with all the seasons, I continue to grow with every sunrise and sunset.

Eventually, I reach the bridge. I have undertaken many highs and lows, and now I have a choice. I can step across to meet my Angel, knowing that I will be totally safe and nurtured,
or I can stay a little longer. I can help others across, as their journeys are now also nearing the end. Either choice is awarded with
a rainbow like aura. I can wear it with honour.

Every step I have taken
Every choice that I have made
Every task I have undertaken

They have all lead me to this bridge, *The Bridge to Heaven.* I am worthy and I now choose to step onto the bridge confidently. I shine like a 'beacon of light'. Others coming up the path can see me shining. The light encourages them to continue along with their journey.

The rewards at the bridge, the Light, the Angel and Heaven, they are for everyone!
When you have reached the bridge you have reached Heaven. Heaven is not a place; Heaven is a state of being. A state of serenity, peace, calm and stillness.

Keep walking today and see the bridge in your sights.

Printed in Great Britain
by Amazon.co.uk, Ltd.,
Marston Gate.